FIELD GUIDE TO

Orchids
of North America

from Alaska, Greenland, and the Arctic
south to the Mexican border

John G. Williams
&
Andrew E. Williams

Illustrated by Norman Arlott

Foreword by Roger Tory Peterson

UNIVERSE BOOKS
New York

For Helen Hirschbein of Cedarhurst, New York
and
Frances P. Evans of Houston, Texas

without whose encouragement, support, and active
assistance this book would not have been written
or published

Published in the United States of America in 1983 by Universe Books
381 Park Avenue South, New York, N.Y. 10016

© text 1983 John G. Williams & Andrew E. Williams
© illustrations 1983 Norman Arlott

83 84 85 86 87 10 9 8 7 6 5 4 3 2 1

Printed in Italy

Library of Congress Cataloging in Publication Data
Williams, John George, 1913-

Field guide to orchids of North America.

Bibliography: p.
Includes index.
1. Orchids—North America—Identification.
2. Botany—North America. I. Williams, Andrew E.
II. Arlott, Norman. III. Title.
QK495.O64W463 1983   584'.15'097   82-23677
ISBN 0-87663-415-3

CONTENTS

North America

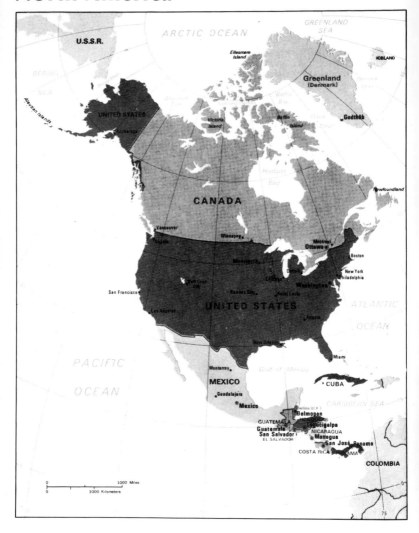

FOREWORD by Roger Tory Peterson

It comes as a surprise to many of us to learn that Orchidaceae is the second largest family of plants in the vegetable kingdom, numbering between 15,000 and 35,000 species, depending on which authority is consulted. Yet the species are by no means commonplace. They enjoy a mystique that transcends that of any other family of wild flowers. Their rainbow colors, bizarre shapes and patterns beguile the eye. Their curious adaptations to life forces and the environment intrigue the imagination.

Most people think of orchids mainly in terms of cattleyas, cymbidiums, and other flamboyant blooms of the florists' trade; they are unaware that some species are so small and modest that they may escape the notice of all but the most sharp-eyed botanist. Orchids are to be found on every continent except Antarctica. Absent only from the polar regions, they have adapted to almost every environment, from hot, moist jungles to parched deserts and cool tundra, and from sea level to altitudes above timberline in the higher mountains.

A great many tropical orchids are epiphytic, anchoring themselves to the rough trunks and outstretched limbs of forest trees where they take much of their nourishment from the humid air. Those in temperate zones, such as the ones dealt with in this book, which covers North America north of the Mexican border, are mainly terrestrial. Only in Florida are many of the epiphytic species to be found.

An orchid may scatter as many as two or three million seeds, so minute as to be like dust in the wind. To germinate and grow, the infant plant must somehow form an intimate partnership with fungi in and around its roots, enabling it to take food from decaying material in the soil. For two to four years a terrestrial orchid may remain as a leafless underground shoot before it sees the light of day. Some species such as the twayblades may take another ten years before they flower.

Although a few species are structurally adapted to pollinate themselves, most orchids rely on their seductively colored lips to lure insects to perform the rites of pollination. Some, such as the bee-orchids, *Ophrys*, and certain tropical orchids have lips that mimic bees or wasps and scents that stimulate males of these insects to attempt sexual union with them. During this pseudocopulation pollen is transferred to the stigma of the plant and the reproductive cycle is triggered. The variations on this theme are many. In most orchids, however, the attraction of the flowers to insects is in terms of food, not of sex. But one ponders the evolutionary processes that have made pollination so complicated or specialized. An extreme example is an orchid in Madagascar that has such a long nectar spur that it can be probed and fertilized only by a single species of insect, a sphinx moth with a proboscis more than twelve inches long.

These peculiar adaptations interested Charles Darwin who had already come to grips with the origin of species through natural selection. In 1862 he published a book on *The Various Contrivances by which Orchids are Fertilized by Insects*, a work that was reissued in 1877 with many additional details.

A conservation note about these vulnerable plants is in order. There is no longer need to collect and press specimens of orchids for the sole purpose of substantiating records, either in Europe or in North America. A good color transparency of the living plant is really much more satisfactory; it takes up less room and gives more lasting pleasure. Such photographs can be taken *in situ*, using either available light or controlled flash. In today's world few orchids can afford the attrition imposed by the vasculum and the plant press. They should be looked at long and appreciatively, perhaps photographed, and then left where they are growing.

6

John Williams, the senior author of this book, might be described as one of those rarities, a true naturalist of the old school. He is not solely an ornithologist, a lepidopterist, or a botanist, but rather the sum of all these and much more. He is aware of the total environment and knows intimately its various components. His son Andrew has followed in his footsteps. As junior author of this guide he augmented the material collected over the years by his father.

In looking over the fine illustrations by Norman Arlott I am reminded of spring and summer days among tranquil surroundings in the wild places of our North American continent. There I have encountered and been entranced by many of our wild orchids. You too, as a naturalist, will find many of these species. This book will help you put names to them.

Roger Tory Peterson

INTRODUCTION

During recent years two monumental and lavishly illustrated publications detailing the wild flowers of North America have appeared, both under the patronage of the New York Botanical Garden. These are the 15-volume work, *Wild Flowers of the United States* by Harold William Rickett, and Carlyle A. Luer's *Native Orchids of Florida* and *Native Orchids of the United States and Canada excluding Florida*.

The publication of these outstanding and beautiful books is most timely, coinciding with the fast-awakening appreciation of our earth's flora and fauna, the knowledge of humanity's interrelationship with all other life forms, and awareness of the urgent need to conserve and protect our fast-disappearing heritage. Already the books have drawn attention to the diversity and beauty of North American wild flowers and the very real dangers of extinction that face so many species. The books have only one drawback: the size and weight of the volumes preclude their being taken into the field and used to identify a particular wild flower in situ. This explains the aim of the present book, *Field Guide to the Orchids of North America*. This and its companion volume, *A Field Guide to the Orchids of Britain and Europe*, have been written expressly for use in the field, to aid in the identification of growing plants, and so to avoid the necessity of picking or digging up any specimens.

In this field guide to the North American orchids the layout and nomenclature—the latter updated in accordance with recent botanical trends—mainly follow the pattern set by D. S. Correll in his *Native Orchids of North America*. All the 177 species of orchid found north of the Mexican border are illustrated, together with most of the generally recognized geographical races and individual varieties. For speedy reference, the text to each appears on the page facing the illustration. The illustrations are the work of the young British artist, Norman Arlott, and are models of botanical accuracy and aesthetic appeal. In painting the plates Norman Arlott worked largely from field notes and color photographs taken by the junior author, Andrew Williams, who in 1971–72 traveled extensively in the United States and in Canada. We wish to take this opportunity to thank the many persons, too numerous to mention individually, who assisted him during his journeys.

The future of many orchids in North America, and this applies equally to other parts of the world, is most insecure. Man's continuing takeover of more and more of the earth's surface has already destroyed or altered many wildlife habitats, and no plant is more vulnerable to habitat disturbance than the orchid. In Florida especially, several species that were not uncommon two or three decades ago have now become very rare and may have disappeared altogether.

We would appeal to all users of this book never to pick, uproot, or attempt to transplant any wild orchid. Instead we urge the use of the camera to capture the beauty of an orchid plant growing among natural surroundings. Such a collection of photographs will afford you constant pleasure and also the satisfaction of making a personal contribution to conservation. With these provisos we wish you good orchid hunting. Certainly your travels in search of orchids will take you to regions where you will learn the meaning of the words "the tranquility of a wild place."

It is the authors' pleasure to acknowledge the help received during the planning, field work, and writing of this book. Above all we are indebted to artist Norman Arlott who worked steadfastly under our direction and endured constructive criticism to produce the plates which illustrate this book; Herbert Bijur of the New York Botanical Garden has tendered his valuable advice; John Bull of the American Museum of Natural History and Mrs. Edith Bull have given enthusiasm and courtesy; Harry N. Darrow has taken me to orchid habitats in New York State; Adrian Dignan has been a tower of strength, providing photographic records of the illustrations in case of loss—and I shall always be grateful to him for taking me to a locality where I first saw that splendid plant, the Moccasin Flower, within sight of New York's skyscrapers; Julian and Kathy Donahue have taken me to localities in California rich in insects and wild flowers; Mrs. Mary Dyer of Ontario showed me my first Showy Lady's Slipper orchids in Canada; Paul Elkin has acted as courier extraordinary in carrying the orchid paintings between England and New York; John Farrand of New York, Al Gilbert of Connecticut and William K. Glekbarg of Santa Monica, California, have all helped with advice and hospitality; Helen Hirschbein has helped me to visit many parts of the Americas from Trinidad to Maine and discovered orchid colonies for me in many places; Bengt Jacobsson of Goteborg, Sweden, has helped me with his knowledge of northern orchids. In California, Lloyd and Julie Kiff of the Western Foundation of Vertebrate Zoology have afforded me constant hospitality and introductions to friends who could help me; Richard and Norma Mastin took me to the high mountains of southern California and to parts of the Californian coast where hummingbirds sometimes drew my attention from orchids; John and Irene Metcalf of Leicester have brought me orchid specimens from Nova Scotia and elsewhere in Canada; Professor Russ Mumford of Purdue University, West Lafayette, Indiana, has accorded me advice, and Frances Evans of Texas has suggested orchid haunts in that state; Dr. and Mrs. Charles Noback of Columbia University showed me orchids of several species; Dr. and Mrs. Ralph Schreiber and Dr. Charles Hogue of the Los Angeles County Museum have all helped me during visits to California; John Serrao, the Greenbank Sanctuary naturalist, in Tenafly, New Jersey, has conducted me through the nature sanctuary he preserves; Derek and Daphne Spindlow of Toronto, Canada, extended me generous hospitality and obtained Canadian orchid photographs; Dr. Randolph L. Peterson of the Royal Ontario Museum and his colleagues have helped me in many ways. To the staff of Universe Books, especially Louis Barron and Sarah Montague, we record our appreciation of their help and advice. Lastly I would say thank you to the many persons not listed to whom I am indebted for kindnesses and hospitality in different parts of the United States and Canada—my co-author and I are most grateful.

The Recognition of an Orchid

Orchids belong to the great group of flowering plants termed Monocotyledons, those plants which on germination of the seed possess only one embryo leaf (cotyledon) as opposed to the two which appear in seedlings of the other division, the Dicotyledons. Members of the Monocotyledon group include the orchids, lilies, amaryllids, irises, and related families.

An orchid flower may be recognized by the number and arrangement of its perianth segments—the three similar outer segments called *sepals*, and the three inner called *petals*. The median petal, known as the lip or *labellum*, is often larger than the two lateral petals and is modified in structure and more brightly colored. In many orchids there is a hollow, nectar-producing *spur* at the base of the *labellum*. Projecting from the center of the orchid flower is a thickened structure known as the *column*, combining the male and female organs of reproduction. At or near the top of the column are the *anthers*, the male section of the organ containing the pollen grains. These are grouped in masses, normally two to four, called *pollinia*. Below the anthers is the upper female portion of the column, the *stigma*, a depressed and often sticky surface to which the pollen grains adhere during pollination. In many orchids, interposed between the anthers and the stigma, is a structure called the *rostellum*. Evolved from an infertile stigma, this serves to inhibit self-fertilization, by preventing the pollen grains reaching the stigma of the same flower. Below the stigma, beneath the perianth, is the *ovary*, containing myriads of tiny ovules, which after fertilization develop into vast numbers of extremely small seeds. The ovary itself expands into an egg-shaped or cylindrical capsule.

The possession of a column and the modified median petal, the lip, distinguish an orchid from all other flowers. An additional character, shared with many other Monocotyledons, is that the leaf veins in orchids are parallel.

Reproduction

Orchids have two main methods of maintaining their numbers—by vegetative multiplication from tubers and root buds, and by production of seeds. There is also a third method: In the case of the tiny Bog Orchid *(Malaxis paludosa)* small projections known as bulbils grow at the tips of the leaves and break off to form new plants.

Most orchids rely upon insects, especially members of the Hymenoptera and Lepidoptera, to help the fertilization of their flowers. When an insect in search of nectar visits an orchid flower it comes in contact with the viscidium, a sticky disk connected by a stalk to the pollinia. The viscidium adheres to the insect, taking with it the pollinia which are carried on to another flower, so ensuring cross-fertilization.

A few orchids are routinely self-pollinated, the projecting pollinia fragmenting so that pollen grains reach the stigma. Self-pollination can occur in various other orchids normally pollinated by insects. Where a flower has not been visited by the normal insect pollinator, the pollinia stalks shrink, as the flower withers, pulling the pollen masses away from the anthers to hang forward above the stigma. Wind movement is then sufficient to bring the pollen into contact with the stigma, and self-fertilization is achieved.

Region Covered

This book describes and illustrates all the species and many of the subspecies and varieties of orchids found in North America north of Mexico, including Alaska, Canada, the Canadian arctic, and western Greenland.

How to Use the Book

A simplified key to the orchid genera will enable the user of this book to narrow the identification to genus, after which a perusal of the text and illustrations will enable a name to be given to most orchid specimens. There are additional keys to the species in the larger genera—*Cypripedium, Platanthera, Listera, Malaxis,* and *Spiranthes.* While most orchids will be identified with the aid of this book, there will be times, especially in the case of such large and difficult genera as Spiranthes and when hybrid plants are encountered, that an individual plant may defy classification except by a botanist specializing in the group in question.

How to Use the Keys

The keys to genera and to species are not foolproof, especially in dealing with the difficult Ladies' Tresses Orchids *(Spiranthes).* The possession of a magnifying glass is often essential, since many of the features used in identification are very small. I would also point out that the beginner may find the keys harder to follow than the species descriptions and illustrations in the main part of the book, since the keys presuppose some botanical knowledge on the part of the user.

Briefly, the keys act in a sequence of elimination. Starting at 1 on each key, the user makes up his mind which of (usually) two possible alternative descriptions the specimen most resembles, and then proceeds to that part of the key indicated by the numeral on the right. By this method the user should arrive at a genus or species which can then be checked against the text descriptions and illustrations.

John G. Williams

KEY TO GENERA OF NORTH AMERICAN ORCHIDS

1   Orchids terrestrial in habit   2
    Orchids epiphytic in habit   40

2   Orchids saprophytic, lacking chlorophyll or green leaves   3
    Orchids not saprophytic, with green leaves or green bractlike scales on a
       green stem   5

3   Flowers, stem, and bracts white; leaves absent   *Cephalanthera* (p. 54)
    Flowers, stem, and bracts brownish, purple, or yellowish; leaves absent   4

4   Lateral sepals free at base   *Hexalectris* (pp. 110–12)
    Lateral sepals united at base, forming a mentum
       Corallorhiza (pp. 112–14)

5   Leaves normally absent or completely withered during flowering   6
    Leaves normally present during flowering   11

6   Inflorescence a solitary flower   *Arethuṣa* (p. 64)
    Inflorescence a few- to many-flowered spike   7

7   Flowers short pedicellate; corolla more or less tubular; inflorescence
       frequently spiraled   *Spiranthes* (part) (see pp. 17–19)
    Flowers long pedicellate; corolla usually spreading; inflorescence a loose
       raceme, not spiraled   8

8   Flowers without spur   *Aplectrum* (p. 108)
    Flowers with spur from base of lip   9

9   Spur broad and conical; inflorescence few-flowered   *Galeandra* (p. 108)
    Spur slender   10

10   Leaves ovate in basal rosette, withered by flowering; flowers symmetrical
       Piperia (part) (p. 48)
    Leaf solitary, withered by flowering; flowers asymmetrical with petal
       overlapping dorsal sepal   *Tipularia* (p. 96)

11   Flowers medium-sized or large with inflated slipper-shaped lip   12
    Lip not inflated or slipper-shaped   13

12   Solitary basal leaf; flower usually solitary; lip pouch-shaped with pair of
       obscure anterior spurs   *Calypso* (p. 96)
    Stem with two or more leaves; flowers one to many; lip inflated and slipper-
       shaped   *Cypripedium* (see p. 14)

13   Leaf solitary   14
    Leaves more than one   22

14   Leaf basal   15
    Leaf borne on stem   19

15   Leaf with long stalk   *Centrogenium* (p. 82)
      Leaf without long stalk   16

16   Leaf broad, elliptic, or ovate   17
      Leaf narrow, grasslike   18

17   Lip entire; flowers greenish yellow to white
                                  Platanthera (part) (see pp. 14–15)
      Lip three-lobed; flowers pink, mauve, or purplish; lip spotted
                                              Amerorchis (p. 32)

18   Lip directed upward; flowers open wide, pink or sometimes white
                                          Calopogon (pp. 64–66)
      Lip lowermost; flowers green with mauve lip, not opening fully
                                          Basiphyllaea (p. 98)
      (Some plants possess two or even more leaves; see no. 24.)

19   Inflorescence normally a solitary flower   20
      Inflorescence a many-flowered spike   21

20   Lip with fringed crest   *Pogonia* (p. 58)
      Lip with papillose crest   *Cleistes* (p. 57)

21   Flowers with spur, greenish yellow
                                  Platanthera (part) (see pp. 14–15)
      Flowers very small, without spur, greenish to reddish
                                  Malaxis (part) (see pp. 16–17)

22   Leaves mainly basal   23
      Leaves mainly borne on stem   34

23   Leaves more or less erect   24
      Leaves in basal rosette   26

24   Leaves two to four, grasslike; corolla tubular; inflorescence spiraled;
         flowers white   *Spiranthes* (part) (see pp. 17–19)
      Inflorescence not spiraled; flowers green with mauve lip, not opening
         fully   *Basiphyllaea* (p. 98)
      Leaves two, elliptic or ovate   25

25   Lip widest below middle; column very short; flowers green or reddish
                                          Malaxis (part) (see p. 17)
      Lip widest above middle; column elongated; flowers green to mauve-tinted
                                          Liparis (part) (p. 94)

26   Lip directed upward; spur absent   27
      Lip directed downward; spur absent   29
      Lip directed downward, spur present   30

27   Flowers very small, floral sections less than 3 mm. long   28
      Flowers small, floral sections more than 3.5 mm. long; flowers white with
         greenish tinge   *Ponthieva* (p. 68)

28   Bracts on stem small and close-fitting; flowers pink   *Prescotia* (p. 68)
     Bracts on stem foliaceous; flowers white and green   *Cranichis* (p. 68)

29   Lip not deeply hollowed; leaves green
                                        Spiranthes (part) (see pp. 17–19)
     Lip deeply hollowed; leaves green with white veining
                                                    Goodyera (pp. 82–84)

30   Leaves two, elliptic; flowers pink with white lip   *Galearis* (p. 30)
     Leaves two or more; flowers not pink and white   31

31   Two pollinia widely separate; lip divided into three slender lobes; flowers
         green   *Habenaria* (pp. 32–48)
     Two pollinia close together above spur opening; flowers greenish
                                                    Piperia (part) (p. 48)
     Leaves plicate (pleated, not smooth), basal   32
     Leaves plicate, borne on stem   34
     Leaves smooth, borne on stem   35

32   Leaves two, with long stems concealed by sheaths; flowers with spur,
         white   *Govenia* (p. 108)
     Leaves two or more; spur absent   33

33   Flowers pink; lip crested   *Bletia* (p. 116)
     Flowers greenish purple and red   *Eulophia* (p. 118)

34   Flowering stem and inflorescence branched; flowers greenish white
                                                    Tropidia (p. 86)
     Flowering stem not branched; inflorescence a simple raceme; flowers
         greenish or reddish   *Epipactis* (pp. 52–54)

35   Leaves two, borne opposite, halfway up stem   *Listera* (see p. 16)
     Leaves not opposite   36

36   Leaves forming whorl on top of stem   *Isotria* (p. 58)
     Leaves not forming whorl   37

37   Leaves borne along stem; spur present   38
     Leaves borne along stem; spur absent   39

38   Spur small, bag-shaped; flowers green-tinged red; lip straplike, three-lobed
         at apex   *Coeloglossum* (pp. 32–34)
     Spur long; flowers pink, mauve, and white, spotted
                                                    Dactylorhiza (p. 32)
     Spur bulbous; flowers white, tinged greenish yellow
                                                    Erythrodes (pp. 85–86)

39   Perennial with fibrous stems, leaves many, lanceolate   *Zeuxine* (p. 86)
     Annual with small delicate stems; leaves bractlike or oval
                                                    Triphora (pp. 54–56)

| 40 | Epiphytic orchid, leafless when in flower | | 41 |
| | Epiphytic orchid, with leaf or leaves | | 43 |

| 41 | Plant very small, roots 1 mm. wide | *Harrisella* (p. 126) | |
| | Plant larger, roots about 5 mm. wide | | 42 |

42	Flowers small in many-flowered raceme, greenish to orange		
		Campylocentrum (p. 126)	
	Flowers large, whitish, borne singly	*Polyrrhiza* (pp. 127–28)	

| 43 | Plant a climbing vine | *Vanilla* (pp. 60–62) | |
| | Plant not a climber | | 44 |

| 44 | Plant forming pseudobulbs | | 45 |
| | Plant not forming pseudobulbs | | 53 |

| 45 | Flowering shoot arising from apex of pseudobulb | | 46 |
| | Flowering shoot arising from side or base of pseudobulb | | 47 |

46	Lip with distinct column foot forming a mentum; flowers greenish		
		Polystachya (p. 106)	
	Lip without distinct column foot; flowers yellowish or mauve, spotted		
		Encyclia (pp. 104–6)	

| 47 | Leaves plicate; pseudobulbs large and spindle-shaped; flowers yellow or green, spotted with purple | *Cyrtopodium* (pp. 118–20) | |
| | Leaves folded lengthwise; pseudobulbs not large or spindle-shaped | | 48 |

48	Two leaves rising from apex of pseudobulb; flowering stem pendent		
		Bulbophyllum (pp. 115 16)	
	Single leaf rising from apex of pseudobulb		49
	Pseudobulb surrounded by leaf sheaths		50

| | Leaf solitary; flowering stem pendent | *Macradenia* (p. 126) | |
| | Leaf solitary; flowering stem not pendent | *Oncidium* (pp. 122–24) | |

50	Inflorescence short, single-flowered; lip entire; flowers yellow		
		Maxillaria (p. 120)	
	Inflorescence elongated, few- or many-flowered; lip entire		51

51	Sepals and petals extremely long and slender; lip entire		
		Brassia (pp. 121 – 22)	
	Sepals and petals short; lip entire	*Leochilus* (p. 124)	
	Lip two- or three-lobed		52

| 52 | Lip two-lobed; flowers pink | *Ionopsis* (p. 120) | |
| | Lip three-lobed; flowers not pink | *Oncidium* (part) (pp. 122–24) | |

53   Pseudobulbs absent; leaf solitary; leaf sheaths fringed with hairs, dilated at
         apex; flowers maroon-red; plant extremely small
                                                           Lepanthopsis (p. 88)
         Pseudobulbs absent; leaf solitary; leaf sheaths smooth, not dilated at
         apex   54
         Leaves more than one   55

54   Inflorescence many-flowered; flowers yellowish white
                                                           Pleurothallis (pp. 8 7 – 88)
         Inflorescence one- or two-flowered; flowers greenish
                                                           Restrepiella (p p. 8 7 – 88)

55   Leaves basal; flowers pink   *Tetramicra* (pp. 97-98)
         Leaves borne along stem; flowers yellowish, brownish, or purple
                                                           Epidendrum (pp. 98–102)

KEY TO THE GENUS CYPRIPEDIUM

1   Margin of lip-pouch opening incurved   2
      Margin of lip-pouch opening not incurved   *C. guttatum* (p. 26)

2   Leaves two, at base of stem; lip-pouch opening longitudinal, narrow
                                                          C. acaule (p. 20)
      Leaves two or more, borne on stem; lip-pouch opening oval   3

3   Leaves two, borne high on stem; flowers clustered   *C. fasciculatum* (p. 26)
      Leaves two or more, borne along stem   4

4   Lateral sepals united, at least at base, below lip; lip pouch oval   5
      Lateral sepals free and spreading, not united below lip; lip pouch with
         conical projection below   *C. arietinum* (p. 20)

5   Lip pouch yellow or yellowish; petals long and slender, usually twisted
                                                          C. calceolus (p. 22)
      Lip pouch white; petals long and slender, usually twisted   6

6   Dorsal sepal about equal to lip in length   *C. candidum* (p. 24)
      Dorsal sepal much longer than lip   *C. montanum* (p. 28)
      Petals ovate to lanceolate, not twisted, usually same length as or shorter
         than lip   7

7   Lip small and white, less than 2 cm. long   8
      Lip larger, more than 2 cm. long, pink or (rarely) white
                                                          C. reginae (p. 30)

8   Flowers one or two, borne at top of stem   *C. passerinum* (p. 28)
      Flowers three to ten, sometimes more, borne along stem; bracts
         foliaceous   *C. californicum* (p. 24)

KEY TO THE GENUS PLATANTHERA

1	Lip fringed or serrated in varying degrees		2
	Lip not fringed or serrated		9
2	Lip entire		3
	Lip three-lobed		5
3	Flowers white; lip deeply fringed	*P. blephariglottis* (p. 34)	
	Flowers white; lip shallowly serrated	*P. integrilabia* (p. 36)	
	Flowers yellow or orange		4
4	Spur longer than ovary and pedicel	*P. ciliaris* (p. 36)	
	Spur equal to or shorter than ovary and pedicel	*P. cristata* (p. 36)	
5	Lip three-lobed; flowers white, greenish white, or cream-colored		6
	Lip three-lobed; flowers mauve		7
6	Petals broad	*P. leucophaea* (p. 40)	
	Petals narrow	*P. lacera* (p. 40)	
7	Lobes of lip deeply fringed		8
	Lobes of lip finely serrated	*P. peramoena* (p. 44)	
8	Anther cells close together above spur orifice	*P. psycodes* (p. 44)	
	Anther cells divergent, on each side of spur orifice	*P. grandiflora* (p. 44)	
9	Anther cells parallel; lip entire		10
	Anther cells parallel; lip three-lobed		11
	Anther cells divergent		12
10	Lip directed upward; flowers white	*P. nivea* (p. 42)	
	Lip directed downward, slightly toothed; flowers yellow	*P. integra* (p. 40)	
	Lip directed downward, concave, rounded; flowers green; spur very short; range Aleutians to Washington	*P. chorisiana* (p. 34)	
11	Lip deeply three-lobed	*P. albida* (p. 34)	
	Apex of lip shallowly three-lobed	*P. clavellata* (p. 36)	
12	Center of lip with prominent protuberance	*P. flava* (p. 38)	
	Lip without prominent protuberance		13
13	Leaf normally solitary		14
	Leaves normally two or more		15
14	Lip linear; spur same length as lip	*P. obtusata* (p. 42)	
	Lip elliptic; spur longer than lip	*P. tipuloides* (p. 34)	
15	Leaves two, basal, opposite		16
	Leaves two or more, sub-basal or borne along stem; spur equal to lip in length		17

16   Stem without bracts   *P. hookeri* (p. 38)
       Stem with one or two lanceolate bracts   *P. orbiculata* (p. 42)

17   Flowers white; lip noticeably wider at base   *P. dilatata* (pp. 36–38)
       Flowers greenish or yellowish green; lip linear   18

18   Lip with small basal protuberance   *P. limosa* (p. 42)
       Lip without small basal protuberance   *P. hyperborea* (pp. 38–40)
       (Note: In *P. hyperborea* var. *purpurascens* the spur is shorter than the lip.)
       Spur not equal to lip in length   19

19   Column small, less than half the length of dorsal sepal; spur shorter than
           lip, thickened with double bulbous tip   *P. stricta* (p. 46)
       Column larger, more than half the length of dorsal sepal; spur slender,
           longer than lip   *P. sparsiflora* (p. 46)

KEY TO THE GENUS LISTERA

1   Lip straplike or dilated at tip; lobes, if present, rounded at tips; flowers
         green or yellowish green   2
     Lip deeply bilobed; lobes slender and pointed; flowers green or reddish   7

2   Lip straplike, approximately equal in width from base to apex   3
     Lip much broader at apex than at base   4

3   Base of lip with small projecting lobes (auricles) curving behind column
                                                                 L. auriculata (p. 50)
     Base of lip with small projecting lobes (auricles) curving away from
         column   *L. borealis* (p. 50)

4   Lip with short basal stalk (claw)   *L. convallarioides* (p. 52)
     Lip sessile   5

5   Lip pointing downward from angle near base; apex bilobed with small
         tooth between lobes   *L. ovata* (p. 52)
     Lip directed outward, not angled   6

6   Lip broadly bilobed at apex with small tooth between lobes
                                                                   L. smallii (p. 52)
     Lip rounded at apex or very slightly notched   *L. caurina* (p. 50)

7   Lip with pair of slender projections (horns) near base
                                                                   L. cordata (p. 52)
     Lip without slender projections near base   *L. australis* (p. 50)

KEY TO THE GENUS MALAXIS

1	Leaf normally solitary	2
	Leaves normally two, sometimes more	7
2	Lip directed downward	3
	Lip directed upward	6
3	Lip distinctly three-lobed	4
	Lip entire	5

4 Central lobe of lip shorter than lateral lobes   *M. unifolia* (p. 92)
  Central lobe of lip much longer than lateral lobes   *M. monophyllos* var.
      brachypoda (p. 91)

5 Inflorescence in cluster at top of stem; flower pedicels 1 cm. long
                                                         M. corymbosa (p. 90)
  Inflorescence borne along slender stem; flower pedicels 3 mm. long
                                                         M. ehrenbergii (p. 90)

6 Lip apex acuminate; flower pedicels 1 cm. long   *M. tenuis* (p. 92)
  Lip apex shallowly three-lobed or notched; flower pedicels 2 mm. long
                                                         M. macrostachya (p. 92)

7 Lip directed upward; distinctly three-lobed; range Aleutian Islands
                                          M. monophyllos var. *diphyllos* (p. 91)
  Lip directed upward, entire   8

8 Plant very small, usually under 10 cm. tall; grows in sphagnum bogs;
      flowers green to yellowish green   *M. paludosa* (p. 92)
  Plant larger, up to 40 cm. tall; flowers greenish brown to reddish
                                                         M. spicata (p. 92)

KEY TO THE GENUS SPIRANTHES
(Note: Based on both botanical characters and distribution)

1 Flowering spike not noticeably spiraled; flowers often brightly colored;
      distribution southern, subtropical   2
  Flowering spike variously spiraled; flowers white, often tinged with green
      or yellow; distribution mainly temperate regions   10

2	Flowers relatively large and brightly colored	3
	Flowers smaller and mainly white, green, and yellow	7

3 Flowers relatively large and colored; leaves usually withered and absent
      during flowering; lip with short basal stem (claw)   4
  Lip without basal stem (claw)   5
  Leaves usually present during flowering   6

4   Flowers pale pink with green lines; lip constricted in middle; distribution
     Texas   *S. durangensis* (p. 70)
     Flowers white with green stripes; lip not constricted in middle; distribution
     Arizona and Texas   *S. michuacana* (p. 76)

5   Flowers large, green; distribution Florida
                                              S. lanceolata var. *luteoalba* (p. 82)
     Flowers large, orange-red; distribution Florida   *S. lanceolata* (p. 82)

6   Leaves usually present during flowering; flowers red; distribution Flori-
     da   *S. lanceolata* var. *paludicola* (p. 82)
     Leaves usually present during flowering; flowers cinnabar red; distribution
     Texas   *S. cinnabarina* (pp. 80–82)

7   Lip with large basal projections   8
     Lip with basal projections very small or absent; distribution Florida
                                                            S. polyantha (p. 78)

8   Lip apex broad, shallowly three-lobed; distribution Florida
                                                          S. cranichoides (p. 70)
     Lip apex narrowed, three-lobed; flowers white with green stripes;
     distribution Florida   *S. costaricensis* (p. 72)
     Lip entire   9

9   Lip with red spot in center; distribution Arizona to Texas
                                                        S. parasitica (pp. 76–78)
     Lip without red spot; distribution Florida   *S. elata* (p. 72)

10   Flower spike closely spiraled; flowers in several parallel lines   11
     Flower spike either with flowers on one side of stem (secund) or spiraled;
     flowers normally in single line   17

11   Flowers small; lip 9 mm. long or less   12
     Flowers larger; lip longer than 9 mm.   14

12   Flowers white or yellowish without contrasting color on lip   13
     Flowers white with bright yellow center; distribution northeastern
                                                             S. lucida (p. 76)

13   Flowers white, flowering in fall; distribution southeastern
                                                             S. ovalis (p. 76)
     Flowers yellowish, flowering in spring and summer; distribution western
                                                          S. porrifolia (p. 80)

14   Lip more or less constricted near center   15
     Lip ovate, not constricted near center   16

15   Flowers white; lip slightly constricted near center; distribution north-
     eastern   *S. cernua* (p. 70)
     Flowers white; lip strongly constricted near center; distribution northern
                                                        S. romanzoffiana (p. 80)

16 Leaves withered, absent during flowering; distribution midwestern
    S. magnicamporum (pp. 70 – 72)
    Leaves present during flowering, extending some way up stem; distribution southeastern *S. odorata* (p. 70)
    Leaves ovate, usually withered during flowering; flowers white with green center; distribution eastern and southeastern
    S. lacera var. *gracilis* (p. 74)

17 Leaves linear or lanceolate   18
    Leaves ovate, often withered at flowering   24

18 Hairs of pubescence with pointed tips; lip with yellow center; distribution eastern *S. vernalis* (p. 80)
    Hairs of pubescence with clubbed tips   19

19 Flowers white; leaves present during flowering   20
    Flowers yellowish or with yellow center to lip   21
    Flowers white; lip with green center; distribution southeastern
    S. tortilis (p. 80)

20 Lip ovate, apex rounded; veined with green; distribution eastern and southeastern *S. praecox* (p. 78)
    Lip oblong, truncate; distribution southern Arizona
    S. graminea (p. 78)

21 Lateral sepals free   22
    Lateral sepals appressed to other floral parts; flowers pale yellow; distribution northeastern *S. ochroleuca* (pp. 70 – 72)

22 Flower spike strongly spiraled   23
    Flower spike secund or loosely spiraled; flowering November, December; distribution southeastern *S. longilabris* (p. 76)

23 Flowers white, lip with yellow center; flowering spring and summer; distribution southeastern *S. laciniata* (p. 74)
    Flowers white, lip with pale yellowish center; flowering late summer and fall; distribution northeastern *S. intermedia* (p. 78)

24 Plant small, usually under 25 cm. tall; strongly spiraled; flowers white, very small, glabrous; distribution eastern and southeastern
    S. tuberosa (p. 74)
    Plants larger, usually over 30 cm. tall   25

25 Lip with green center; distribution northeastern
    S. lacera var. *lacera* (p. 74)
    Lip with yellow center; distribution southeastern
    S. brevilabris (p. 74)

SPECIES DESCRIPTIONS AND PLATES

Lady's Slippers *Cypripedium*

Perennials, 15–120 cm.; root system a creeping rhizome; leaves two or more, normally broadly elliptic or oval; bracts leaflike; flowers large and showy; perianth composed of four or five spreading segments; lateral sepals connate in many species, pointing downward behind lip; lip large and pouch-shaped, inflated; no spur; column stout, projects forward and slightly downward, partially closing lip aperture; two fertile anthers, one on each side of column; column covered by staminode.

Genus *Cypripedium* contains between twenty and thirty species distributed in temperate and cold regions of North America, Asia, and Europe, with ten species occurring in North America, north of Mexico.

Moccasin Flower *Cypripedium acaule* Aiton

15–40 cm., terrestrial, pubescent; leaves two, opposite, elliptic, deeply pleated, rising from base of stem; flower solitary with leaflike bract; dorsal sepal from greenish to dark purple, lanceolate, lateral sepals completely fused, projecting downward behind lip; petals ovate-lanceolate, downy at base, sometimes twisted, mauve to purple; lip an elongated pouch with longitudinal aperture, pink or magenta, often with darker veins; albino forms occur; staminode ovate, greenish to mauve; ovary subsessile.

Easily recognized by its two basal leaves and elongated pink lip. Distribution northeastern states, north to Ontario and Newfoundland, northwestward to Saskatchewan and Alberta, south to South Carolina, Georgia, Tennessee, and Alabama. Habitat extremely variable, growing in both hardwood and conifer woodlands, in swamps and bogs, in dense woodland along streams, and on coastal sand hills. Still a common species in many areas. Flowers from mid-April in the south of its range, continuing until July in northern areas.

Ram's Head Lady's Slipper *Cypripedium arietinum* R. Brown in Aiton

10–30 cm., terrestrial, pubescent; leaves three to five, borne along stem, narrowly elliptic to ovate-lanceolate, obtuse to acute; flower solitary at tip of stem with broad leaflike bract; sepals all free, laterals not connate, purplish, more or less streaked with green; petals similar to lateral sepals; lip funnel-shaped, conical below, whitish with purplish veining, darker below; staminode suborbicular, mauve-green; ovary subsessile; flower fragrant.

Very local and uncommon, found in northeastern United States, north to Quebec, Ontario, and Manitoba, south to Wisconsin, Illinois, and Minnesota. Grows both in sphagnum swamps and on wooded slopes on limestone. Flowers in May and June.

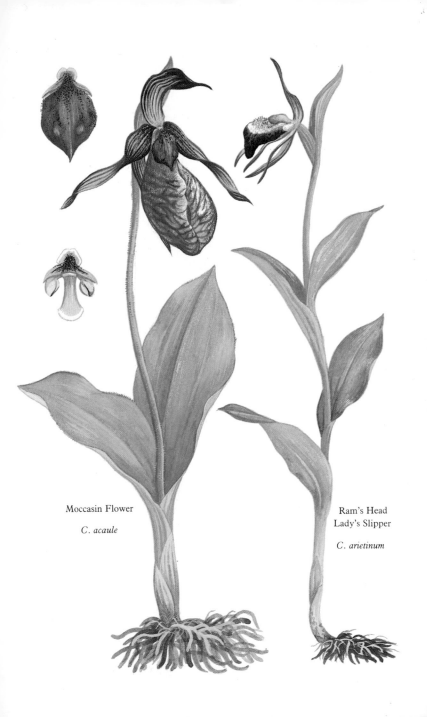

Moccasin Flower

C. acaule

Ram's Head
Lady's Slipper

C. arietinum

Yellow Lady's Slipper *Cypripedium calceolus* Linnaeus var. *pubescens* (Willdenow) Correll
15–60 cm., terrestrial, pubescent; leaves three to five, elliptic to ovate, borne on stem; flowers one or two, large and showy; floral bract leaflike, green; dorsal sepal ovate-lanceolate, yellowish green with or without brownish veining, lateral sepals united nearly to apex; petals long and slender, twisted; lip an oval pouch 3–6.5 cm. long, bright yellow, speckled reddish on inside; staminode triangular, yellow with red spots; ovary subsessile.

An extremely variable species, the nominate form of which occurs in Europe and Asia. Two additional varieties found in North America: var. *parviflorum* (Salisbury) Fernald and var. *planipetalum* (Fernald) Victorin and Rousseau. The former a diminutive form with lip only 2–2.5 cm. long; petals long and very twisted. The var. *planipetalum* has lip 2–3 cm. long, with relatively short and broad petals that are flat, not twisted; sepals and petals normally yellowish green.

Easily recognized by its yellow pouch. Var. *pubescens* widely distributed in northeastern United States, north to Quebec and Newfoundland, west to Yukon, British Columbia, and Washington, south to Georgia, Alabama, Louisiana, and Texas. Grows in a variety of habitats from sphagnum bogs and swamps to humid woodlands and open deciduous woods and rocky wooded slopes. Flowers from May to July in the North.

Var. *parviflorum* grows in northeastern United States and adjacent areas in Canada. Habitat swamps and bogs. Flowers during May and June.

Var. *planipetalum* occurs mainly on limestone barrens in northern Newfoundland, eastern Quebec, and extreme eastern Ontario. Flowers in July.

var. *parviflorum*

Yellow Lady's Slipper

C. calceolus var. *pubescens*

var. *planipetalum*

California Lady's Slipper *Cypripedium californicum* A. Gray
25–120 cm., terrestrial, pubescent; leaves five to ten, alternate, broadly ovate to ovate-lanceolate; inflorescence elongated, flowers three to twelve; bracts leaflike; dorsal sepal elliptic, greenish yellow, lateral sepals united almost to apex, greenish yellow; petals broad, yellow to green; lip a rounded sac, 1.5–2 cm. long, white, sometimes tinged with pink or lightly spotted purple above aperture; staminode broadly ovate, white or white with green markings; ovary pedicellate.
Easily recognized by its long raceme of white-lipped flowers. Very uncommon with restricted distribution in southwestern Oregon and northern California. Grows in damp situations along wooded mountain streams. Flowers from May to July depending on altitude.

Small White Lady's Slipper *Cypripedium candidum* Muhlenberg ex Willdenow
15–40 cm., terrestrial, sparsely pubescent; leaves three to five, elliptic-lanceolate, sheathing the stem; inflorescence a solitary flower; floral bract leaflike, sheathing the ovary; dorsal sepal about same length as lip, green, often tinged brown; lateral sepals fused nearly to apex; petals long, slightly twisted, green, often with brownish markings; lip an oval pouch, white, sometimes lightly veined mauve; staminode ovate, yellow with sparse mauve markings; ovary subsessile.
A small, white-lipped species that can be distinguished from the Mountain Lady's Slipper by its relatively short sepals. Also their distributions are quite different: *C. montanum* is found in the mountains of the western United States; Small White Lady's Slipper occurs in northeastern states, north to Ontario, locally in Manitoba, south to Missouri and Kentucky, perhaps most frequent in Michigan. Species normally grows in boggy meadows. Flowers from late April to June in northern part of its range.

California
Lady's Slipper

C. californicum

Small White Lady's Slipper

C. candidum

Clustered Lady's Slipper *Cypripedium fasciculatum* Kellogg ex S. Watson
6–20 cm., terrestrial, pubescent; leaves two, broadly elliptic, opposite, borne high on stem; inflorescence two to four flowers in short, crowded raceme; floral bracts lanceolate, leaflike; dorsal sepal lanceolate to ovate, greenish heavily marked purplish brown, lateral sepals fused almost to apex; petals ovate, similar to sepals; lip small, 1–1½ cm. long, a rounded pouch, greenish, mottled purplish brown; staminode pale green; ovary slender, stalked.
Can be recognized by its paired leaves high on the stem and its crowded head of two to four brownish green flowers. Restricted distribution in Montana, Wyoming, Idaho, Colorado, and Utah, west to Washington, Oregon, and northern California. An uncommon and local species growing at moderate altitudes in moist or dry coniferous forest in the mountains, in acid soils. Flowers from April to July, depending on altitude and locality.

Spotted Lady's Slipper *Cypripedium guttatum* Swartz
10–25 cm.; terrestrial, pubescent; leaves two, elliptic, subopposite; inflorescence a solitary flower, white with irregular purplish or brownish spots or blotches; bract large and leaflike; dorsal sepal broadly ovate, acute and deeply concave, lateral sepals united almost to apex; petals spreading, wide at base; lip a globose sac with a large rounded orifice the sides of which are everted, not incurved; staminode ovate, yellow with purple spots; ovary pedicellate.
Can be recognized by its lip aperture margins, which are everted, not incurved, and by its purple-blotched white flowers. A northern species found locally in Alaska and the Yukon, sometimes in abundance. Grows in open birch forests and similar habitats. Flowers during June and July.
Var. *yatabeanum* (Makino) Pfitzer in Engler replaces typical plants on the Alaskan peninsula, in the Aleutians, and on Kodiak Island. Pale yellowish or greenish blotched with brown; petal tips spatulate. Grows in exposed situations in seepage areas and boggy grasslands. Flowers during June and July.

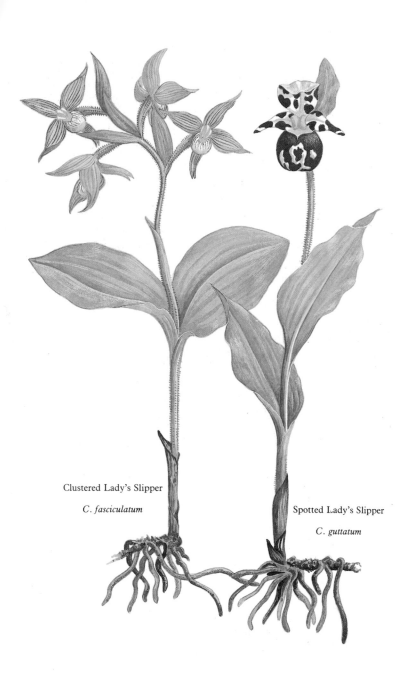

Clustered Lady's Slipper

C. fasciculatum

Spotted Lady's Slipper

C. guttatum

Mountain Lady's Slipper *Cypripedium montanum* Douglas ex Lindley

25–70 cm., terrestrial, pubescent; leaves four to six, ovate-lanceolate; inflorescence one to three flowers on upper part of stem; bracts leaflike; dorsal sepal ovate-lanceolate, undulant, longer than lip, greenish suffused with purple, lateral sepals fused nearly to apex; petals very long, slender, and twisted, purplish; lip an oval pouch, white sometimes veined purple at base, 2–3 cm. long; staminode ovate, yellow with purple spots; ovary subsessile.

Can be distinguished from the Small White Lady's Slipper by its much longer sepals, which exceed the lip in length. Confined to northwestern regions from southern Alaska, British Columbia, Vancouver Island, and western Alberta, south to Montana, Idaho, Wyoming, and northern California. Habitat mountain areas, growing on subalpine slopes, open woodland, and scrub at moderately high altitudes. Flowers from May to July.

Sparrow's Egg Lady's Slipper *Cypripedium passerinum* Richardson

12–35 cm., terrestrial, pubescent; leaves three to five, ovate-lanceolate; inflorescence usually a solitary flower; bract leaflike; dorsal sepal broad and concave, yellowish green, lateral sepals united nearly to apex; petals linear-oblong, spreading, white; lip an oval sac, 1–2 cm. long, white, speckled red-brown at base and sometimes below; staminode ovate, white to yellowish at apex, speckled red-brown; ovary subsessile, thick.

Can be distinguished from other white-lipped Lady's Slipper orchids by its short, blunt sepals and petals. Far northern distribution from Alaska east to southern end of Hudson Bay, south to northwestern Montana. Habitats include moist coniferous forests, wooded ravines, and littorals of streams and lakeshores. Flowers during June and July.

Mountain Lady's Slipper

C. montanum

Sparrow's Egg Lady's Slipper

C. passerinum

Showy Lady's Slipper *Cypripedium reginae* Walter
35–90 cm., terrestrial, densely pubescent; leaves 3–7, ovate, sheathing stem at base; inflorescence normally one or two flowers, large and showy; bract leaflike, sheathing the ovary; dorsal sepal broadly ovate, white, lateral sepals fused behind lip, white; petals oblong-elliptic, white; lip a pouch-shaped sac with shallow furrows, rose-pink streaked white, or mostly white; staminode ovate, white with rose-purple spots, 2½—5 cm. long.
Easily recognized by its contrasting white sepals and petals and rose-colored lip. Ranges through the northeastern states, north to Newfoundland, west to southern Manitoba and southeastern Saskatchewan, south to the mountains of South Carolina and Tennessee. Habitat open areas around margins of bogs and swamps, sphagnum bogs, and wet woodland. Flowers from late May to August in extreme North.

Showy Orchis *Galearis*

Previously included in the genus *Orchis*. Characterized by very short rhizome and fleshy roots; lacks tubers; two basal leaves; floral bracts much longer than flowers. One species in North America, another in Japan.

Showy Orchis *Galearis spectabilis* (Linnaeus) Rafinesque
(Syn. *Orchis spectabilis* Linnaeus)
7–35 cm., terrestrial, glabrous; leaves two, basal, subopposite, elliptic; inflorescence a loose raceme of up to fifteen flowers; floral bracts large and foliaceous; sepals and petals connivent, forming hood over column, pink or purplish; lip white or tinged pink, entire, ovate with more or less wavy margin; column stout, 7 × 4 mm.; spur stout, 7 mm. long; ovary stout, pedicellate.
A common forest and woodland species, recognized by its purplish hood and pale lip and its pair of broad basal leaves. Range northeastern states, north to Quebec and Ontario, south to Missouri and mountains of South Carolina, Georgia, and Alabama, west through the central and lake states. A woodland orchid, favoring beech and maple woods and sheltered ravines. Flowers from April in southern areas to July in north of its range.

Showy Lady's Slipper

C. reginae

Showy Orchis

G. spectabilis

Small Round-Leaved Orchis *Amerorchis*

Previously classified under *Orchis*. Characterized by its solitary leaf and its lack of tubers.

Small Round-Leaved Orchis *Amerorchis rotundifolia* (Banks) Hultén

(Syn. *Orchis rotundifolia* Banks ex Pursh)

10–35 cm., terrestrial, glabrous; leaf solitary, basal, ovate; inflorescence a loose raceme of up to fifteen flowers; bracts lanceolate, about 1 cm. long; sepals and petals pink to white, dorsal sepal and petals connivent, forming hood over column, lateral sepals spreading; lip white with red or mauve markings, three-lobed, central lobe broad, sometimes bilobed; spur slender, 5 mm. long; column short, 3 mm.; ovary thick, pedicellate.

Easily recognized by its solitary leaf, hood, and spreading lateral sepals. A high northern species ranging from Alaska across Canada to Labrador, Newfoundland, and southwestern Greenland; rare southward to Montana, Wisconsin, Michigan, and New York. Habitat open tundra and limestone barrens and farther south coniferous forest on limestone soil. Flowers from May to August in the north of its range.

Fischer's Orchid *Dactylorhiza*

Mainly an Old World group represented in North America by two species. Differs from genus *Orchis* in having palmate tubers instead of rounded entire tubers.

Fischer's Orchid *Dactylorhiza aristata* (Fischer) Soó

(Syn. *Orchis aristata* Fischer ex Lindley)

10–40 cm., terrestrial, glabrous; leaves two to five, green, normally unspotted; inflorescence a densely flowered raceme of up to thirty flowers that vary in color from deep mauve, pink, or salmon red to white; bracts lanceolate, tinged purple-brown, longer than flowers; sepals and petals forming hood, lateral sepals more or less spreading; lip entire or three-lobed, mauve to white, with or without mauve spotting; spur conical, 7–15 mm. long; ovary thick, pedicellate; column stout, 5 × 2 mm.

Differs from *D. maculata* in its slender, acuminate sepals and petals. Range Alaska and the Aleutian Islands where it grows in meadows, in boggy seepages, and on grassy slopes; locally abundant. Flowers late May to early July.

Var. *kodiakensis* Luer & Luer filius from Kodiak Island has heavily spotted leaves, deep magenta flowers, and dark purple bracts.

The common European Spotted Orchis, *Dactylorhiza maculata* (Linnaeus) Soó, recorded in recent years in a lakeshore habitat near Timmins, Ontario. Similar to Fischer's Orchid, but sepals and petals not acuminate.

Habenaria Orchids

Following present-day trends in classification, the *Habenaria* group is divided into four genera: *Habenaria,* which is confined to the extreme southeastern United States; *Coeloglossum,* a monotypic genus with a northern range; *Piperia,* with three species, all from the western United States; and *Platanthera,* which is the largest group.

Frog Orchid *Coeloglossum*

Often included in the genus *Habenaria*. Tuber or tubers palmate as in *Dactylorhiza;* characterized by long bracts and straplike lobes with central tooth between them. Widespread in Europe, Asia, and North America.

Frog Orchid *Coeloglossum viride* (Linnaeus) Hartman

10–60 cm., terrestrial, glabrous; leaves two to five, varying from elliptic to lanceolate, sheathing the stem; inflorescence moderately dense to lax, five to twenty flowers; bracts long or very long, longer than flowers; flowers green more or less suffused with red; sepals and petals incurved forming a rounded helmet; lip oblong, straplike, with three lobes at apex; spur small and rounded; ovary thick, about 6 mm.; column short and stumpy.

(Continued on next text page)

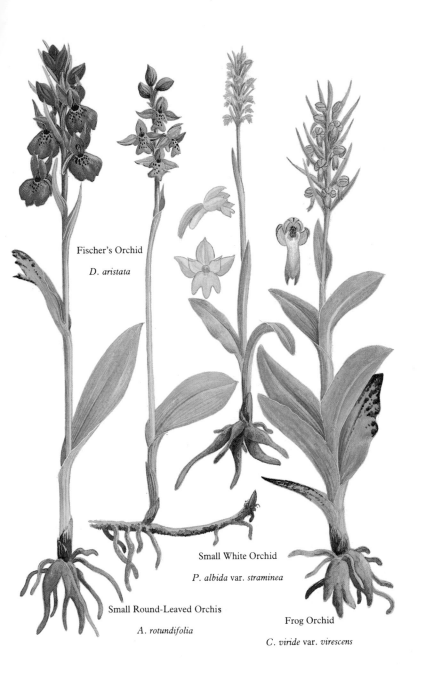

Fischer's Orchid

D. aristata

Small White Orchid

P. albida var. *straminea*

Small Round-Leaved Orchis

A. rotundifolia

Frog Orchid

C. viride var. *virescens*

Identified by its long floral bracts and straplike lip. Typical form with relatively shorter bracts occurs from northern Alaska across northern Canada to Hudson Bay and Labrador. Farther south, from southern Alaska across Canada to Newfoundland and in northwestern and northeastern United States, it is represented by plants with very much longer bracts, var. *virescens* (Muhlenberg) Luer (syn. *bracteata* Muhlenberg in Willdenow). Habitat tundra meadows, seepage areas, woods, and thickets. Flowers from May in the south of its range to August in the north.

Small White Orchid *Platanthera albida* (Linnaeus) Lindley
var. *straminea* (Fernald) Luer
(Syn. *Leucorchis albida* [Linnaeus] E. May ex Schur)
(Syn. *Habenaria albida* [Linnaeus] R. Br. var. *straminea* [Fernold] Morris & Edmes)
5–35 cm., terrestrial, glabrous; leaves two to five, sheathing stem; inflorescence a dense spike, many-flowered; flowers yellowish green to yellowish white; bracts longer than ovary; sepals and petals incurved to form hood; lip ovate, apex deeply three-lobed; spur short and thick; ovary short; column 1 × 1 mm. with anther cells parallel.
Typical *albida* occurs in Europe and has white flowers. In North America found only in southern Greenland and the limestone barrens of Cape Norman, Newfoundland. Flowers during July and August.

Behring Island Habenaria *Platanthera tipuloides* (Linnaeus) Lindley
var. *behringiana* (Rydberg) Hultén
(Syn. *Habenaria behringiana* [Rydberg] Ames)
7–18 cm., terrestrial, glabrous; leaf normally solitary, sometimes two leaves, sub-basal, elliptic; large foliaceous bract above leaf; inflorescence moderately lax; bracts longer than flowers; dorsal sepal forming hood with petals, lateral sepals spreading, greenish yellow; lip elliptic, obtuse, yellow; spur slender, longer than ovary; ovary stout, stalked; column stubby, 2 × 2 mm.
In North America confined to western Aleutians and other islands in Bering Sea where it grows on damp open hillsides. Flowers during July and August.

Chamisso's Orchid *Platanthera chorisiana* (Chamisso) Reichenbach
(Syn. *Habenaria chorisiana* Chamisso)
6–20 cm., terrestrial, glabrous; two to four sub-basal leaves with bract above; inflorescence a moderately lax raceme of minute green flowers; bracts longer than flowers; sepals and petals strongly incurved forming a hood; lip entire, broad, rounded at apex, fleshy; spur very short; ovary short, thickened; column very short, 1 × 1 mm.
A small-flowered green orchid that occurs in the Aleutian Islands and south to Vancouver Island, rarely to the state of Washington. Grows among grasses and in mossy turf where it is often overlooked. Flowers during July and August.

White Fringed Orchid *Platanthera blephariglottis* (Willdenow) Lindley
(Syn. *Habenaria blephariglottis* [Willdenow] Hooker)
30–60 cm., terrestrial, glabrous; leaves two to three, elliptic to lanceolate, keeled; bracts above; inflorescence twenty to thirty white flowers in fairly lax raceme; floral bracts slender, about same length as ovary; dorsal sepal concave, lateral sepals reflexed; petals slender, somewhat incurved; lip entire, ovate, deeply fringed; spur 15–20 mm. long; ovary slender; column thick, 3 × 3 mm.; anther sacs separate.
Identified by white flowers and fringed lip. Range, northeastern United States, north to Newfoundland, west to Michigan. Grows in bogs and damp meadows. Flowers from June to August.

(Continued on next text page)

var. *conspicua*

Monkey-Face

P. integrilabia

Chamisso's Orchid

P. chorisiana

White Fringed Orchid

P. blephariglottis

Behring Island
Habenaria

P. tipuloides
var. *behringiana*

Yellow-Fringed Orchid

P. ciliaris

Var. *conspicua* (Nash) Luer is a more robust plant that grows to 1 m. tall with a spur 30–40 mm. long. Southeastern in distribution; occurs from New Jersey pine barrens south along Atlantic seaboard and Gulf Coast. Flowers from June in the north of its range to October in Florida.

Monkey-Face, *Platanthera integrilabia* (Correll) Luer, previously considered a variety of *P. blephariglottis*. Differs from that species in having a spatulate lip that is finely serrated along the margin but not fringed. Occurs in North Carolina, Georgia, Kentucky, Tennessee, Alabama, and Mississippi. Habitat bogs, swamps, and along streams. Flowers during August and September.

Yellow Fringed Orchid *Platanthera ciliaris* (Linnaeus) Lindley
(Syn. *Habenaria ciliaris* [Linnaeus] R. Brown in Aiton)
24 cm.—1 m., terrestrial, glabrous; leaves two to four, lanceolate, keeled; stem with bracts above leaves; inflorescence a relatively dense to lax many-flowered raceme with up to sixty orange flowers; bracts slender, about same length as ovary; dorsal sepal broad and concave, lateral sepals broad, reflexed; petals toothed at apex, incurved; lip entire, deeply fringed; spur slender, down-curved, 25–30 mm. long; ovary slender, orange; column 3 × 3 mm.; two opposite anther cells.
Differs from Crested Yellow Orchid in its much longer spur and larger flowers. An eastern species, distribution from southern Ontario south through Atlantic states to Texas, west through central and lake states to Michigan, Wisconsin, Illinois, Missouri, and Arkansas. Grows in swamps, bogs, thickets along streams, wet pine barrens, seepage areas, wet meadows, and moist upland forest. Flowers from late June in south of range to September in north.

Small Green Wood Orchid *Platanthera clavellata* (Michaux) Luer
(Syn. *Habenaria clavellata* [Michaux] Sprengel)
15–35 cm., terrestrial, glabrous; leaves one, rarely two, keeled, with few bracts above; inflorescence a short, lax raceme of three to fifteen pale yellowish green flowers; bracts as long as ovary; dorsal sepal and petals incurved, lateral sepals slightly spreading; lip oblong, slightly trident at apex; spur 10 mm. long with dilated tip; ovary stout; column short and broad, 1 × 1.5 mm.
Recognized by its single leaf, borne just below the middle of a slender stem. Eastern in range from Newfoundland, southern Quebec, and Ontario, south through Atlantic states to Florida and Texas, west through central and Great Lakes states to Minnesota, Iowa, Missouri, and Arkansas. Grows in swampy forests, along wooded streams and creeks, in bogs, and on margins of lakes; locally common. Flowers from June to August.

Crested Yellow Orchid *Platanthera cristata* (Michaux) Lindley
(Syn. *Habenaria cristata* [Michaux] R. Brown)
18–80 cm., terrestrial, glabrous; leaves two to four, lanceolate, keeled; many bracts above leaves; inflorescence a relatively dense many-flowered raceme with up to eighty small orange flowers; bracts lanceolate, shorter than ovary; dorsal sepal and petals incurved, lateral sepals spreading; petals toothed; lip ovate, entire, deeply fringed; spur slender, 8 mm. long; ovary slender; column short and stubby; 2 × 2 mm.; two opposite anther cells.
Distinguished from similar *P. ciliaris* by smaller flowers and spur shorter than lip. Range northeastern states, south through Atlantic states to Florida and eastern Texas. An uncommon species growing in damp coniferous woodland, seepage areas, and damp meadows. Flowers from late June to late July, sometimes in August and early September.

Leafy White Orchid *Platanthera dilatata* (Pursh) Lindley
(Syn. *Habenaria dilatata* [Pursh] Hooker)
30 cm.–1 m., terrestrial, glabrous; leaves numerous, up to twelve, linear-lanceolate, becoming bractlike above; inflorescence an elongated, many-flowered spike; flowers white; dorsal sepal and petals incurved, lateral sepals spreading; lip dilated at base, narrowing at apex; spur equaling or slightly longer than lip; column short and thick; ovary slightly longer than lip.
A very variable species in which typical plants are brilliant white with relatively short spurs. Often hybridizes with *P. hyperborea*. Range from Alaska and Aleutian Islands across Canada to Newfoundland and southwestern Greenland. In the western states, south through Washington, Oregon, California, Nevada, Utah, and northern New Mexico, east through the lake states, rarely to Pennsylvania and New England. Grows in bogs, marshes, and damp meadows; locally abundant in Arctic regions. Flowers from June to August.

(Continued on next text page)

Small Green Wood Orchid

P. clavellata

Crested Yellow Orchid

P. cristata

Leafy White Orchid

P. dilatata

Florida Habenaria

H. distans

Var. *leucostachys* (Lindley) Luer differs in having a much longer spur up to 20 mm. long. Occurs locally from British Columbia south to California.

Var. *albiflora* (Chamisso) Ledebour has a conical spur much shorter than the lip. Occurs in southern Alaska, south through British Columbia to Montana, Idaho, Wyoming, Utah, and Colorado. Flowers from late May to August.

Florida Habenaria *Habenaria distans* Grisebach

14–30 cm., terrestrial, glabrous; leaves five to six in basal rosette; narrow bracts on stem above; inflorescence lax, five to fifteen yellowish green flowers; floral bracts lanceolate, shorter than flowers; dorsal sepal ovate, concave, lateral sepals narrow, reflexed; petals yellowish green, deeply bifurcated, the upper division under edge of dorsal sepal, the lower division very slender, upcurved; lip pale green, deeply three-lobed, central lobe straplike, lateral divisions slender and curving upward; spur 17 mm. long, club-shaped toward apex; column with two separate anther sacs; ovary slender, ascending.

Can be recognized by its basal leaf rosette and thickened, clublike spur. A rare species in North America, confined to a few localities in southwestern Florida. Grows in dense stands of hardwood forest. Flowers from mid-August to September.

Southern Rein Orchid *Platanthera flava* [Linnaeus] Lindley

(Syn. *Habenaria flava* [Linnaeus] R. Brown in Sprengel)

15–50 cm., terrestrial, glabrous; leaves one to four, lanceolate; inflorescence a lax spike of ten to forty yellowish green flowers; bracts lanceolate, as long as or longer than ovary; dorsal sepal ovate, concave, lateral sepals ovate, spreading; petals broad, yellowish green; lip broad, dentate, with small lateral lobes and a small tubercle at base; spur longer than lip, thickened toward apex; ovary stout, sessile; column 1.5×2 mm. with divergent anther sac on either side.

Can be recognized by its divergent anther sacs and lip tubercle. Widely distributed in southeastern states from Virginia to eastern Texas. Habitat open woodland, thickets, moist meadows, and swampy areas at margins of lakes and streams. Flowers from March to October. In the northeastern states, from Missouri to Nova Scotia, its place is taken by var. *herbiola* (R. Brown) Luer, with a narrower, longer lip and larger, more numerous leaves. Most frequent in wet woodland. Flowers from May to August.

Hooker's Orchid *Platanthera hookeri* (Torrey) Lindley

(Syn. *Habenaria hookeri* Torrey in A. Gray)

18–40 cm., terrestrial, glabrous; leaves two opposite, basal, broadly elliptic; inflorescence a lax spike of up to twenty-five yellowish green flowers; floral bracts lanceolate, slightly longer than ovary; dorsal sepal ovate, tapering, lateral sepals oblong, spreading or reflexed; petals slender and tapering; lip triangular, tapering; spur slender, 15–25 mm. long; column 3×3 mm., anther sacs diverging, tubercle above stigma; ovary slender, pedicellate.

Recognized by its two oval basal leaves and spike of yellowish green flowers. *P. orbiculata*, which also has a pair of basal leaves, has white flowers. Distribution northeastern and Great Lakes states and adjacent areas of Canada, west to Manitoba, east to Nova Scotia. An uncommon species, locally frequent, in both deciduous and coniferous forest and woodland in drier areas. Flowers from May to August.

Northern Green Orchid *Platanthera hyperborea* (Linnaeus) Lindley

(Syn. *Habenaria hyperborea* [Linnaeus] R. Brown in Aiton)

10–40 cm., terrestrial, glabrous; leaves three to six, oblong to linear-lanceolate, bractlike above; inflorescence a fairly dense- to lax-flowered spike of yellowish green to green flowers; floral bracts longer than ovary; dorsal sepal and petals incurved to form hood, lateral sepals spreading; lip broadly lanceolate, obtuse; spur curved, shorter than ovary; column short; anther sacs divergent; ovary stout, up to 10 mm. long.

Species is variable, but typical plant can be recognized by its leafy stem and fairly dense flower spike of small yellowish green to green flowers. Readily hybridizes with *P. dilatata*. Distribution from Alaska and Aleutian Islands across Canada to Newfoundland and southern Greenland; from the northeastern states through the lake states to Minnesota, west and southwest to South Dakota, Nebraska, Colorado, New Mexico, Arizona, California, Oregon, and Washington. Habitat moist tundra and moorland, bogs, damp woods, and thickets. Flowers from June to September.

(Continued on next text page)

Hooker's Orchid

P. hookeri

Southern Rein Orchid

P. flava

Northern Green Orchid

P. hyperborea

Yellow Fringeless Orchid

P. integra

Among the varieties that have been named are the following: Var. *huronensis* (Nuttall) Luer, similar to the typical plant but far more robust, growing to 1 m. tall. From Minnesota, Wisconsin, and southern Ontario east to Nova Scotia, south to northwestern Pennsylvania.

Var. *gracilis* (Lindley) Luer has laxly flowered inflorescence, with a more slender lip. Occurs at high altitudes in mountains of Northwest, north to southern Alaska where it grows in seepage areas and along streams.

Var. *viridiflora* (Chamisso) Luer, another robust form growing to 1 m. tall. Inflorescence dense and many-flowered in most instances. From southern Alaska and the Aleutian Islands.

Var. *purpurascens* (Rydberg) Luer, from higher elevations in the central and southern Rocky Mountains. Characterized by its very short, thick spur, much shorter than lip.

Yellow Fringeless Orchid *Platanthera integra* (Nuttall) Gray ex Beck
(Syn. *Habenaria integra* [Nuttall] Sprengel)

24–60 cm., terrestrial, glabrous; leaves one or two, lanceolate, keeled, with bracts above; inflorescence a dense, many-flowered raceme with thirty to forty bright yellow flowers; floral bracts lanceolate, about same length as ovary; dorsal sepal and petals incurved, forming a hood, lateral sepals spreading; lip entire, oblong, rounded with crenulate margin; spur slender, shorter than ovary; column small, two parallel anther sacs; ovary stout, horizontal.

May be recognized by its yellow flowers, unfringed lip, and parallel anther sacs. A southern species, found locally along Atlantic seaboard from New Jersey pine barrens (rare) to northern Florida to southeastern Texas, also in mountains of Tennessee and North Carolina. Habitat includes acid swamps, seepage areas, and marshy meadows. Flowers from late July to September.

Ragged Fringed Orchid *Platanthera lacera* (Michaux) G. Don
(Syn. *Habenaria lacera* [Michaux] R. Brown)

25–75 cm., terrestrial, glabrous; leaves two to five, elliptic to lanceolate, keeled, with few bracts above; inflorescence a many-flowered rather lax raceme with twenty to forty creamy green flowers; floral bracts lanceolate, slightly longer than ovary; dorsal sepal and narrow petals forming loose hood, lateral sepals spreading; lip tripartite, deeply cut into long filaments; spur slender, up to twenty-three mm. long; column stumpy; anther sacs separate; ovary stout.

Distinguished from *P. leucophaea* by its narrow petals. Distribution northeastern states north to Nova Scotia and Ontario, west through lake states, south to Arkansas, Mississippi, Alabama, Georgia, and South Carolina. Grows locally in swamps, bogs, damp woodland glades, thickets, and seepage areas. Flowers from May in the South to August in the North.

Var. *terrae-novae* (Fernald) Luer, from the barrens and tundra of Newfoundland, is smaller, up to 35 cm. tall, with less deeply cut lip segments; cream-colored flowers. Flowers in July and August.

Prairie Fringed Orchid *Platanthera leucophaea* (Nuttall) Lindley
(Syn. *Habenaria leucophaea* [Nuttall] A. Gray)

20–120 cm., terrestrial, glabrous; leaves two to five, keeled, bracts above; inflorescence a laxly flowered raceme of fifteen to twenty-five creamy white flowers; floral bracts lanceolate, short; dorsal sepal ovate, lateral sepals ovate, spreading; petals broadly spatulate, forming hood with dorsal sepal; lip tripartite, deeply cut into filaments; spur slender, up to 50 mm. long; column 3 × 3 mm.; anther sacs separate; ovary long pedicellate.

Can be distinguished from *P. lacera* by its broadly spatulate petals. Ranges from the lake states west to North and South Dakota, Nebraska, and Kansas, north to southern Ontario, east to Maine. Habitats include damp meadows, lake margins, and sphagnum bogs. Flowers from May to August.

(Continued on next text page)

Ragged Fringed Orchid

P. lacera

Prairie Fringed Orchid

P. leucophaea

Thurber's Bog Orchid

P. limosa

Thurber's Bog Orchid *Platanthera limosa* Lindley

(Syn. *Habenaria limosa* [Lindley] Hemsley)

30 cm.–1.5 m.; terrestrial, glabrous; leaves five to ten, lanceolate, with few bracts above; inflorescence usually a laxly flowered spike of green flowers; floral bracts lanceolate, longer than ovary; dorsal sepal and petals forming hood, lateral sepals spreading or reflexed; lip elliptic-lanceolate, thickened down center with minute tuberosity at base; spur slender, over twice length of lip; column stubby; ovary short, pedicellate.

A locally uncommon species in southern Arizona and southwestern New Mexico; center of abundance in the mountains of Mexico. Grows in bogs, along mountain streams, and in wet forests. Flowers from June to October.

Snowy Orchid *Platanthera nivea* (Nuttall) Luer

(Syn. *Habenaria nivea* [Nuttall] Sprengel)

20–60 cm., terrestrial, glabrous; leaves two to three, lanceolate, keeled; bracts above; inflorescence a dense terminal raceme with twenty to fifty pure white flowers with lips directed upward; floral bracts lanceolate, about same length as ovary; middle sepal pointing downward, ovate, lateral sepals slightly twisted and spreading; petals oblong, obtuse; lip entire, directed upward, slender, bent backward at center; spur straight and slender, 15 mm. long; column very short, yellow; anther sacs separate; ovary stout, horizontal.

The somewhat similar *P. integra* has lip directed downward and yellow flowers. Distribution of *P. nivea* from New Jersey and Delaware south along Atlantic seaboard to Florida, west to Texas. Habitat includes swampy depressions, damp grasslands, pine barrens, and acid bogs. Flowers from May to September.

One-Leaved Rein Orchid *Platanthera obtusata* (Banks ex Pursh) Lindley

(Syn. *Habenaria obtusata* [Banks ex Pursh] Richardson)

8–35 cm., terrestrial, glabrous; leaf solitary, rarely two leaves, tapering to a sheathing base; inflorescence lax, three to seven greenish white flowers; floral bracts about as long as ovary; dorsal sepal ovate, lateral sepals horizontal; petals erect, twisted; lip horizontal or deflexed; spur variable, curved, half as long to as long as ovary; anther sacs slightly divergent; ovary pedicellate.

Can be recognized by its solitary leaf and lax raceme of greenish white flowers. Ranges from Alaska and Aleutian Islands across Canada to Labrador and Newfoundland, south to northeastern states, Illinois, Wisconsin, northern Minnesota, and Montana to Colorado. Habitat includes tundra, barrens, bogs, coniferous forests, and seepage areas along streams and lakeshores. Flowers in July and August.

Round-Leaved Orchid *Platanthera orbiculata* (Pursh) Lindley

(Syn. *Habenaria orbiculata* [Pursh] Torrey)

20–60 cm., terrestrial, glabrous; leaves two, subopposite, basal, broadly rounded, 10 × 8 cm., spreading flat on the ground, silvery beneath; inflorescence a laxly flowered raceme of up to twenty white flowers; floral bracts shorter than flowers; dorsal sepal orbicular, erect, lateral sepals ovate, reflexed; petals ovate-lanceolate, spreading; lip linear-oblong, pendent; spur cylindrical, longer than lip, incurved toward apex; column with a prominent projection on each side; ovary slender, pedicellate.

Hooker's Orchid, which also has two basal leaves, differs in having yellowish green flowers. Distribution of *P. orbiculata* from British Columbia east through the Great Lakes region to Labrador and Newfoundland. An uncommon species found in damp coniferous forests and other forests, in balsam-spruce bogs, and on tundra in Labrador and Newfoundland. Flowers from June to September.

Var. *macrophylla* (Goldie) Luer occurs in northeastern United States, north to Newfoundland. A more robust plant, growing to 60 cm. tall, with larger leaves and flowers twice the size of the typical plant.

P. obtusata

P. orbiculata

var. *macrophylla*

Round-Leaved
Orchid

Snowy Orchid

P. orbiculata

One-Leaved Rein Orchid

P. nivea

P. obtusata

Purple Fringeless Orchid *Platanthera peramoena* A. Gray

(Syn. *Habenaria peramoena* A. Gray)

35–105 cm., terrestrial, glabrous; leaves two to five, elliptic to lanceolate, keeled; bracts above; inflorescence a lax to moderately dense raceme of thirty to fifty mauve to red flowers; floral bracts lanceolate, same length as ovary; dorsal and lateral sepals elliptic, the latter reflexed; petals spatulate; lip three-lobed, the central lobe notched; spur slender, curved, 25–30 mm. long; column thick; anther sacs diverging; ovary slender, pedicellate.

Distinguished from the two Fringed Orchids by its unfringed lip. An uncommon species, local in Illinois, Indiana, Ohio, western New York, western New Jersey south to Mississippi. Grows in damp woods, moist meadows, roadside ditches, and along mountain streams. Flowers from June to September.

Small Purple Fringed Orchid *Platanthera psycodes* (Linnaeus) Lindley

(Syn. *Habenaria psycodes* [Linnaeus] Sprengel)

15–90 cm., terrestrial, glabrous; leaves two to five, elliptic to lanceolate, keeled; bracts above; inflorescence a densely or laxly flowered raceme with thirty to fifty mauve to purple flowers; floral bracts same length as ovary; dorsal sepal elliptic, concave, lateral sepals ovate, spreading; petals erect; lip three-lobed, lobe margins fringed; spur slender, 12–18 mm. long; column short; anther sacs separate but close; ovary short, purplish.

Differs from Large Purple Fringed Orchid by its smaller, less deeply fringed lip. Distribution in northeastern United States, north to Ontario, Quebec, and Newfoundland, west to Iowa, Illinois, and Ohio, south from New Jersey to Georgia. Grows in mountains, swamps, wet thickets, damp meadows, and along mountain streams. Flowers from June to August.

Large Purple Fringed Orchid *Platanthera grandiflora* (Bigelow) Lindley

(Syn. *Habenaria fimbriata* [Dryander] R. Brown in Aiton)

30–120 cm., terrestrial, glabrous; leaves two to six, elliptic, keeled, with bracts above; inflorescence more than 5 cm. thick, laxly or densely flowered, thirty to sixty mauve to purplish flowers; dorsal sepal elliptic, concave, lateral sepals ovate, spreading; petals oblong, erect; lip three-lobed, lobes deeply fringed; spur slender, 25 mm. long; column 4 × 4 mm.; anther cells diverging; ovary 20 mm. long.

Distinguished from *P. psycodes* by much larger size and more deeply fringed lip. Occurs locally in northeastern states, west to Wisconsin and southern Ontario, north to Newfoundland, south in Appalachians to North Carolina. Grows in wet meadows, open swampy woodland, and seepage areas. Flowers from June to August.

Long-Horned Habenaria *Habenaria quinqueseta* (Michaux) A. Eaton

30–60 cm., terrestrial, glabrous; leaves three to seven, ovate to lanceolate; inflorescence a laxly flowered spike with three to fifteen green and white flowers; floral bracts about same length as ovary; dorsal sepal ovate, concave, lateral sepals oblong, spreading; petals white, bipartite, upper division under edge of dorsal sepal forming hood, lower division very slender, curved upward; lip white, divided into three slender lobes; spur slender, 5–10 cm. long; column with two separate anther sacs; ovary slender, ascending.

Can be distinguished by its two-lobed petals, three-lobed lip, and spur up to 10 cm. long. Distribution from eastern South Carolina, Georgia, and Florida, west to Louisiana and southeastern Texas. Grows in pine woodlands, oak flatwoods, hammocks, and sandy areas. Flowers from August in the north of its range to January in the south.

The var. *macroceratitis* (Willdenow) Luer has a longer spur, 12–18 cm. Known from the hammocks of central and northern Florida. Flowers in August.

Small Purple
Fringed Orchid

P. psycodes

P. grandiflora

Purple Fringeless Orchid

P. peramoena

Large Purple
Fringed Orchid

P. grandiflora

Long-Horned Habenaria

H. quinqueseta

Sparsely-Flowered Bog Orchid *Platanthera sparsiflora* (S. Watson) Schlechter
(Syn. *Habenaria sparsiflora* S. Watson)
15–75 cm., terrestrial, glabrous; leaves four to ten, oblong; inflorescence an elongated, laxly flowered spike of green flowers; floral bracts lanceolate, longer than ovary; dorsal sepal ovate, forming hood with petals, lateral sepals spreading or reflexed; lip linear, entire, 6–14 mm. long; spur cylindrical, about as long as lip; column large, about $3 \times 2\frac{1}{2}$ mm.; ovary short, pedicellate, 10 mm. long.
A somewhat variable species, recognized by its tall and slender habit and widely spaced flowers. May be distinguished from *P. hyperborea* var. *gracilis* by its much larger column, usually more than half the length of dorsal sepal. A western species that occurs from Washington south to California, Utah, Colorado, Arizona, and New Mexico. Habitat includes damp hillsides, marshy meadows, and bogs in the western mountains. Flowers from April to September.
Var. *brevifolia* (Greene) Luer from southern New Mexico has a more crowded flower spike.
Var. *ensifolia* (Rydberg) Luer has a very large column that nearly fills the hood, and very slender leaves. Described from mountains in Arizona.

Slender Bog Orchid *Platanthera stricta* Lindley
(Syn. *Habenaria saccata* Greene)
15 cm.–1 m., terrestrial, glabrous; leaves four to ten, oblong to linear-lanceolate, few bracts above; inflorescence a laxly flowered, elongated spike of green flowers; floral bracts longer than ovary; dorsal sepal ovate, forming hood with petals, lateral sepals spreading or reflexed; lip entire, linear-elliptic; spur short, pouch-shaped; column 2×1.5 mm.; ovary short, pedicellate, 10 mm. long.
Similar to several other slender green-flowered orchids, especially some of the *P. dilatata* and *P. hyperborea* groups, but may be identified by its linear or elliptic lip and small pouch-shaped spur. Distribution from Aleutian Islands and southern Alaska south through Washington to northern California, Utah, and Colorado. Locally common in mountains, favoring wet meadows, seepages, and margins of streams. Flowers from May to September.

Water-Spider Orchid *Habenaria repens* Nuttall
10–90 cm., terrestrial to aquatic, glabrous; leaves three to eight, mainly basal, yellowish green, sheathing the stem; inflorescence a densely flowered raceme with up to fifty green to yellowish green spindly flowers; floral bracts longer than ovary; dorsal sepal concave, forming a hood with upper division of petals, lateral sepals spreading; petals greenish white, bipartite, upper division falcate, lower division very slender arching downward; lip greenish white, deeply three-lobed, middle lobe linear, side lobes slender; spur slender, down-pointing, 13 mm. long; column with two separate anther sacs; ovary stout, ascending.
Can be distinguished by its three-lobed lip, mainly basal leaves, and aquatic habitat. Distribution along Atlantic seaboard from southeastern North Carolina to Florida to Texas. Grows in very wet places, often on floating islands of other aquatic plants, also seepages in meadows, lakeshores, hammocks, and ditches. Flowers at almost any time of year.

Water-Spider Orchid

H. repens

Slender Bog Orchid

P. stricta

Sparsely-Flowered Bog Orchid

P. sparsiflora

Straight Habenaria *Habenaria odontopetala* Reichenbach filius

25cm.—1m., terrestrial, glabrous; leaves 5–12, borne alternately along stem; inflorescence usually a laxly flowered raceme of up to sixty yellowish green flowers; floral bracts shorter than ovary; dorsal sepal obovate, concave, lateral sepals oblong, spreading; petals yellow, toothed; lip yellowish green, linear, with pair of small projections at base; spur slender, 25 mm. long; column with 2 distal, parallel anther sacs; ovary slender, ascending.

Can be recognized by its toothed petals. Confined to Florida where it is one of the more common woodland orchids. Grows in both wet and dry habitats. Flowers from September in northern Florida to February in southern Florida.

Piperias *Piperia*

A group of three species previously treated under *Habenaria*, characterized by a basal group of leaves that often disintegrate before the flower spike matures and by the presence of two tubers in the root system. All 3 species confined mainly to western U.S.

Alaska Orchid *Piperia unalascensis* (Sprengel) Rydberg

(Syn. *Habenaria unalascensis* [Sprengel] S. Watson)

25–70 cm., terrestrial, glabrous; leaves 2–4, basal, often disintegrating at time of flowering; bracts above; inflorescence a spike of distantly spaced small yellowish green flowers; floral bracts about same length as ovary; sepals ovate to elliptic, lateral sepals adherent to base of lip; petals ovate-lanceolate; lip ovate-elliptic with central thickening; spur cylindrical, 3–4 mm. long; column short; anther cells parallel; ovary subsessile, 4 mm.

Can be distinguished from *P. elegans* by its shorter spur. Ranges from Aleutian Islands and southern Alaska south to California, east to Montana and Wyoming; also very locally in Nevada, Utah, Colorado, Michigan, southern Ontario, and Anticosti Island. Habitats include forests, open meadowland, rocky hillsides, and tundra. Flowers from April to August.

Elegant Piperia *Piperia elegans* (Lindley) Rydberg

30–90 cm., terrestrial, glabrous; leaves basal, 3–5, usually absent at time of flowering; inflorescence a dense raceme of green flowers; individual flowers similar to those of *P. unalascensis* but with much longer spur.

A western species known from British Columbia, Washington, Idaho, Montana, Oregon, and California. Grows in open woodland, in ravines, and on mountain slopes; most frequent at low altitudes and at sea level. Flowers from July to September.

Var. *elata* (Jepson) Luer is more similar to *P. unalascensis* with a laxly flowered spike but can be distinguished by its long spur.

Coast Piperia

P. maritima

Coast Piperia *Piperia maritima* Rydberg

25–35 cm., terrestrial, glabrous, robust; leaves 3–5, basal, not usually present at flowering, inflorescence a dense, many-flowered cylindrical spike of white flowers marked with green; floral bracts slightly longer than ovary; sepals ovate-elliptic, white-veined with green at base; petals white with basal green stripe; lip ovate, fleshy with thickened central ridge; spur cylindrical, 10–15 mm. long; column short; anther cells parallel; ovary subsessile, 7 mm. long.

Easily distinguished from other Piperias by its densely congested flower spike and mainly white flowers. Occurs along Pacific coast of southwestern Washington, Oregon, and California. Grows in turf right on the coast. Flowers from July to September.

Elegant Piperia

P. elegans

(Continued on next text page)

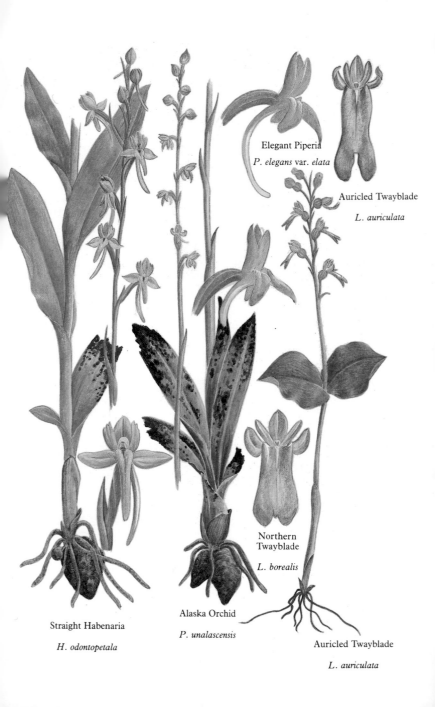

Elegant Piperia

P. elegans var. *elata*

Auricled Twayblade

L. auriculata

Northern
Twayblade

L. borealis

Straight Habenaria

H. odontopetala

Alaska Orchid

P. unalascensis

Auricled Twayblade

L. auriculata

Twayblades *Listera*

Small terrestrial plants with fibrous roots and slender stems; more or less glandular-pubescent; leaves two, opposite or subopposite, borne about middle of stem; inflorescence a lax terminal raceme; lip longer than sepals and petals; column wingless; anther borne on back of column near apex; pollinia 2, powdery.

Auricled Twayblade *Listera auriculata* Wiegand
6–25 cm., terrestrial, glabrous below, pubescent above; leaves 2, opposite, borne above middle of stem, glabrous; inflorescence a laxly flowered raceme of up to 20 pale green or purple-tinged flowers; floral bracts shorter than ovary and pedicel; sepals and petals spreading or reflexed; lip oblong, apex cleft into 2 obtuse lobes; column curved; ovary stout, on pedicel.
Very similar to *L. borealis*, but auricles at base of lip curve toward column. Distribution from around Lake Superior, east across Ontario and Quebec to Newfoundland; south to Maine and New Hampshire. An uncommon species growing along streams and in alluvial soils. Flowers from late June to August.

Northern Twayblade *Listera borealis* Morong
5–25 cm., terrestrial, glabrous below leaves, slightly pubescent above; leaves 2, opposite, above middle of stem; inflorescence lax, up to 20 pale bluish green flowers; floral bracts shorter than ovary; dorsal sepal elliptic, lateral sepals oblong; petals linear; lip oblong, slightly narrowed in middle, apex expanded and divided into 2 lobes with small tooth between; base with diverging auricles; column curved; ovary stout, on pedicel.
Very similar to *L. auriculata*, but auricles at base of lip diverge and center of lip apex is toothed. A northern species ranging from Alaska across Canada to western Newfoundland, south to Lake Superior and Utah. Grows mainly at higher altitudes in both coniferous and hardwood forests and along streams. Flowers in June and July.

Southern Twayblade *Listera australis* Lindley
8–20 cm., terrestrial, finely pubescent on basal leaf sheaths; leaves two, opposite, borne about middle of stem; floral bracts very short; inflorescence lax, five to twenty-five minute greenish purple flowers; dorsal and lateral sepals ovate; petals oblong, recurved; lip linear with distal half split into two slender lobes; base of lip extended into two lobes, one on each side of column; column stumpy; ovary thick, pedicellate.
Similar to *L. cordata* but lacks pair of horns at base of lip. An eastern and southeastern species widely distributed locally from southern Quebec and New York to Florida and eastern Texas; also Tennessee, North and South Carolina, Georgia, and Alabama. In the northern part of its range it favors sphagnum bogs and damp thickets; farther south it may be found in deep shade in wet woods. An uncommon and elusive species. Flowers from January in the South to July in the North.

Northwestern Twayblade *Listera caurina* Piper
5–25 cm., terrestrial, leaves two, opposite, above middle of stem, glabrous below, pubescent above; floral bracts short, about length of ovary; sepals lanceolate; petals linear; lip ovate with two small horns at base, apex rounded with small central tooth; column short; ovary on slender pedicel.
Can be recognized by its lip shape and presence of two small horns at base of lip. Distribution locally from southern Alaska south to northwestern California and Wyoming. Grows in shady coniferous forests. Flowers from June to September.

(Continued on next text page)

Appalachian
Twayblade

L. smallii

Heart-Leaved
Twayblade

L. cordata

Northwestern
Twayblade

L. caurina

Southern Twayblade

L. australis

Broad-Leaved Twayblade

L. convallarioides

Broad-Leaved Twayblade *Listera convallarioides* (Swartz) Nuttall

5–35 cm., terrestrial, stem pubescent; leaves two, opposite, above middle of stem, broadly ovate; inflorescence laxly flowered, up to twenty yellowish green flowers; floral bracts short; dorsal sepal elliptic, lateral sepals lanceolate, curved; petals linear; lip narrowed toward base, apex rounded, shallowly lobed with small central tooth; column curved; ovary stout on slender pedicel.

Can be recognized by broad apex to shallowly lobed lips. Distribution from British Columbia across Canada to Newfoundland, south to northern California, Utah, and Colorado; also Minnesota, Wisconsin, Maine, and Nova Scotia; recorded from Aleutian Islands. Grows in damp, mossy coniferous and mixed forests, bogs, swamps, wet thickets, and peaty barrens. Flowers from June to August.

Heart-Leaved Twayblade *Listera cordata* (Linnaeus) R. Brown in Aiton

5–25 cm., terrestrial; leaves two, opposite, about halfway up stem, ovate to cordate; inflorescence usually a laxly flowered raceme of up to twenty-five minute green and reddish purple flowers; floral bracts minute; sepals and petals ovate to elliptic; lip 3–4 mm. long, linear, apex split into two slender lobes, pair of spreading horns at base; column short and thick; ovary thick on slender pedicel.

Can be recognized by pair of horns at base of lip. Distribution from Alaska across Canada to Newfoundland and southern Greenland; also in northwestern states south to northern New Mexico, and northeastern states to North Carolina. Grows in sphagnum bogs, in coniferous forests, among heather in swamps, subalpine forest, and thickets. Flowers from late May to August.

In the mountains of the western states var. *nephrophylla* (Rydberg) Hulten is found. A more robust plant with leaves and flowers much larger than in typical plants. Flowers green or yellowish green, never reddish. Flowers from June to July in Rocky Mountains.

Appalachian Twayblade *Listera smallii* Wiegand

5–25 cm., terrestrial, glabrous below leaves, pubescent above; leaves two, opposite, about midway on stem; inflorescence a lax raceme of up to fifteen green or brownish green flowers; floral bracts small; sepals lanceolate; petals similar to sepals; lip wedge-shaped, narrower toward base; apex divided into two expanded lobes with small tooth between, base of lip with rounded lobe on each side; column curved; ovary slender, on pedicel.

Can be recognized by two small lobes at base of lip. An uncommon species from the Appalachian Mountains, from Pennsylvania south to Tennessee, Virginia, and North Carolina. Grows in shady forests, among rhododendrons, and in ravines. Most frequent in the north of its range. Flowers in June and July.

The European Common Twayblade, *Listera ovata* (Linnaeus) R. Brown in Aiton, has in recent years been recorded from southeastern Ontario on an island in Lake Huron. This species, 20–60 cm. high, bears a spike of up to fifty flowers. Can be recognized by the base of the lip which is angulated downward; apex divided into two blunt lobes. Ontario plants flower in June and July.

Helleborines *Epipactis*

20 cm.–1 m., rhizomes and fleshy roots but no tubers; stem with evenly spaced leaves; flowers on distinctly twisted stalks, drooping or horizontal; ovary not spirally twisted; perianth segments either spreading or incurved forming a lax hood; lip composed of two sections joined in center, the basal part (hypochile) forming a cup, the apical part (epichile) enlarged into a heart-shaped, triangular, or rounded down-pointing lobe; no spur; column short; rostellum present or absent. The closely related genus *Cephalanthera* has erect, stalkless flowers and a spirally twisted ovary.

Giant Helleborine *Epipactis gigantea* Douglas ex Hooker

20 cm.–1 m., terrestrial, glabrous; leaves four to twelve, ovate-lanceolate, alternate along stem; inflorescence up to fifteen flowers in lax raceme; floral bracts leaflike, lanceolate, longer than flowers; sepals ovate-lanceolate, greenish yellow with reddish purple veining, lateral sepals spreading; petals rose-pink, more or less tinged green; lip three-lobed, divided into two sections by central constriction; hypochile concave with lateral lobes yellowish veined reddish; epichile elongated with apex pink and pair of fleshy orange ridges; column short, anther sac hinged above, green with two pairs of pollinia; ovary curved, pedicellate.

(Continued on next text page)

Broad-Leaved Helleborine

E. helleborine

Giant Helleborine

E. gigantea

Distinguished from *E. helleborine* by its three lobed lip and elongated epichile. A western species ranging locally from southern British Columbia, south to California, Arizona, and New Mexico. Grows along gravelly shores of lakes and rivers, on sandbars in rivers and streams, and in seepage areas. Flowers from March to August.

Broad-Leaved Helleborine *Epipactis helleborine* (Linnaeus) Crantz
(Syn. *Epipactis latifolia* [Linnaeus] Allioni)

35 cm.–1 m., terrestrial, sparsely pubescent; leaves four to ten, broadly oval, often tinged purplish, arranged in spiral up stem; bracts on base of inflorescence longer than flowers, shorter above; inflorescence up to fifty flowers in lax to dense one-sided raceme; flowers opening fully, horizontal or slightly drooping; sepals and petals spreading, broad, green; petals often pinkish violet at base; lip entire, hypochile cup-shaped, reddish brown inside; epichile broadly triangular, recurved apex, greenish white, pink or purplish; two basal protuberances; column short; ovary pedicellate. Distinguished from E. *gigantea* by its entire lip and triangular epichile. An alien species originating in Europe but now not uncommon in the northeastern states from the Great Lakes and southeastern Canada to Maine and south to Missouri. Grows in woodland, ravines, and thickets and on banks of streams. Flowers in June and July.

Phantom Orchid *Cephalanthera*

The genus *Cephalanthera* is mainly a European and Asian group with one species only in North America. The Phantom Orchid is the only member of the genus that is saprophytic. The genus differs from the closely related *Epipactis* in having a sessile, twisted ovary.

Phantom Orchid *Cephalanthera austinae* (A. Gray) Heller
(Syn. *Eburophyton austinae* [A. Gray] Heller)

20–65 cm., terrestrial, saprophytic, leafless, glabrous; a totally white orchid; stem with white sheaths to bracts above; inflorescence a lax raceme of up to twenty white flowers; floral bracts shorter than ovary; sepals and petals elliptic-lanceolate, incurving; lip divided into two sections; hypochile concave with triangular lateral lobes; epichile heart-shaped, curved downward, center with five yellow ridges; column cylindrical with hinged terminal; pollinia two, white; ovary sessile, twisted, erect.

A completely white species except for the yellow epichile ridges, and as such is unmistakable. A western orchid found in the shade of coniferous forests in the mountains of Washington, Oregon, Idaho, and California. Local and uncommon. Flowers from June to August.

Triphora Orchids *Triphora*

Five species of the genus *Triphora* occur in the U.S.; four are confined to Florida, and one has a wider distribution in the East. All are small, succulent, fragile plants with fleshy roots and tubers; leaves alternate. Lip of flower three-lobed with three crests; column simple and free; anther united to apex of column; pollinia in two parallel anther cells.

Three Birds Orchid *Triphora trianthophora* (Swartz) Rydberg
8–25 cm., terrestrial, succulent, glabrous; leaves 2–8, broadly ovate, to cordate, green tinged with purple, margins smooth; inflorescence a loose raceme of 1–6 nodding white or pink flowers, borne on stalks from upper leaf axils; sepals and petals oblanceolate, lateral sepals and petals curved; lip three-lobed, lateral lobes ovate, middle lobe rounded, sinuate, center of lip with 3 parallel green ridges; column cylindrical; anther terminal; ovary slender, pedicellate.

(Continued on next text page)

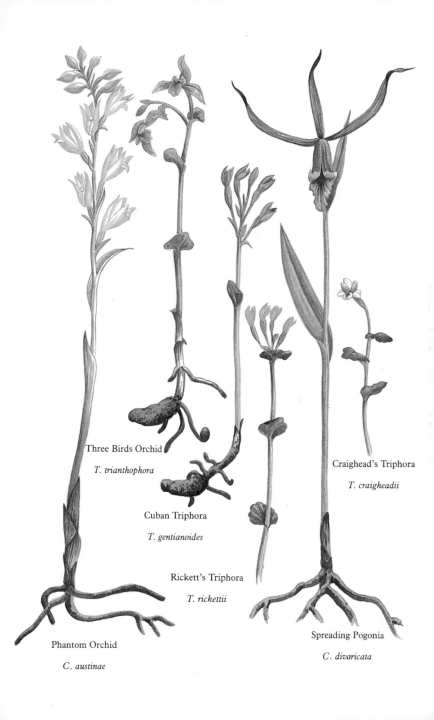

Three Birds Orchid

T. trianthophora

Cuban Triphora

T. gentianoides

Rickett's Triphora

T. rickettii

Craighead's Triphora

T. craigheadii

Phantom Orchid

C. austinae

Spreading Pogonia

C. divaricata

Can be distinguished by its leaves which diverge from the stem and are green on upper and under surfaces, and by its nodding flowers and abaxial lip. Distribution from southern Ontario south through the New England, Great Lakes, and Atlantic states to Florida, west to Texas. Grows on rotting logs and in rich humus in both coniferous and hardwood forests, along wooded streams, and in Florida in low hammocks. Grows from sea level to nearly 2,000 m. in North Carolina. Flowers from July to November.

Cuban Triphora *Triphora gentianoides* (Swartz) Ames and Schlechter
(Syn. *Triphora cubensis* [Reichenbach f.] Ames)
8–20 cm., terrestrial, succulent; leaves 3–10, brownish green, ovate, appressed to stem; inflorescence corymbose with 3–10 erect flowers, yellowish green, borne on elongated stalks from leaf axils; sepals linear-lanceolate, lateral sepals curved; petals similar, pale yellowish green; lip three-lobed, lateral lobes ovate, middle lobe with sinuate margin and, in center, three parallel green ridges; column slender; anther terminal; ovary slender.
Distinguished by leaves appressed to stem and corymbose raceme. In North America confined to a few localities in southern Florida, growing in shade on hammocks; rare. Flowers in late June and July.

Craighead's Triphora
T. craigheadii

Wide-Leaved Triphora
T. latifolia

Rickett's Triphora
T. rickettii

Rickett's Triphora *Triphora rickettii* Luer
8–20 cm., terrestrial, succulent; leaves 5–10, dark green, ovate to cordate with generally wavy margins; inflorescence 1–8 erect, pale yellow flowers borne on short stalks from leaf axils.
Similar to *T. gentianoides* but with leaves diverging from, not appressed to, the stem. Confined to Florida where it is not uncommon. Grows in damp humus in hardwood forests of central and northern peninsular Florida. Flowers from late July to late August.

Wide-Leaved Triphora *Triphora latifolia* Luer filius
4–9 cm., terrestrial, succulent, glabrous; leaves 2–4, green, broadly ovate to reniform, margins smooth; inflorescence a solitary white flower from apex of stem; sepals and petals oblong-lanceolate; lip three-lobed, central lobe undulate, with three green ridges; column slender; anther terminal; ovary slender, pedicellate.
Distinguished by its single white flower and extremely wide leaves. First discovered in 1969. Known only from forest in northern and central Florida; rare. Flowers from July to September.

Craighead's Triphora *Triphora craigheadii* Luer
4–8 cm., terrestrial, succulent, glabrous; leaves 1–4, green above, purple below, broadly ovate to cordate with more or less wavy margin; inflorescence 1–3 flowers, white with magenta and green suffusion; dorsal sepal obovate, lateral sepals and petals ovate, falcate, from greenish white to white with magenta apical markings; lip three-lobed, broadly triangular, white with magenta markings; three ridges in center of lip; column with terminal anther; ovary slender, stalked.
Distinguished by color of leaves and magenta markings on lip. Rare, known only from northwestern Florida. Grows in damp humus in shady forest. Flowers during late June.

Spreading Pogonia *Cleistes*

Previously classified in the genus *Pogonia*. Roots fibrous supporting an erect stem; leaf solitary, inflorescence 1–3 rose-pink flowers; sepals linear, spreading; petals close together over crested lip. One species in southeastern U.S.

Spreading Pogonia *Cleistes divaricata* (Linnaeus) Ames
20–80 cm., terrestrial, erect, leaf solitary, borne halfway up stem; inflorescence a terminal single flower; floral bract leaflike, lanceolate, longer than ovary. Sepals long and slender, spreading, reddish brown to deep purple; petals oblanceolate with tip recurved, pink to white, converged over lip; lip obovate, indistinctly three-lobed, yellowish green veined purple with a rose-red tip; margin crenulate, center with a yellow ridge; column slender with terminal anther; ovary slender, 42 mm. long.
Easily identified by its slender spreading sepals and pink petals that converge over lip. Distribution from New Jersey south to northern Florida and southeastern Texas; also eastern Kentucky and Tennessee. Grows in New Jersey pine barrens, savannas, swamps, bogs, and damp meadows and along streams, from sea level to 1,300 m. in mountains of North Carolina and Tennessee. Flowers from April to June.
Var. *bifaria* Fernald is a smaller, drab-colored form connected by intermediates to the typical plant. Occurs mainly in mountain areas.

Whorled Pogonias *Isotria*

A genus of two species, both confined to eastern United States. Pubescent root system, hollow stem with whorl of five or six leaves; single flower, rarely two, rising from center of the whorl; sepals slender and spreading; petals converged over lip, lip three-lobed with central ridge; column slender with terminal anther.

Whorled Pogonia *Isotria verticillata* (Muhlenberg ex Willdenow) Rafinesque

10–30 cm., terrestrial, glabrous; leaves five or six in whorl at top of purplish stem; leaves erect as bud opens; inflorescence normally a solitary terminal flower; no floral bract; sepals purplish, narrowly lanceolate, up to 50 mm. long, widely spreading; petals greenish yellow, converging over lip; lip three-lobed, lateral lobes edged purple, middle lobe white or yellowish, spreading with wavy margin, center with fleshy ridge; column slender with terminal anther; ovary slender, pedicellate.

Differs from the Small Whorled Pogonia in having flower pedicel at least 12 mm. long and erect leaves as bud opens. Distribution from Great Lakes east to Maine, south to eastern Texas, Louisiana, Mississippi, Alabama, Georgia, and South Carolina. Grows in both wet and dry habitats, sphagnum bogs, woodland, beech forest, and along streams. Flowers from April in the South to August in the North; local and generally uncommon.

Small Whorled Pogonia *Isotria medeoloides* (Pursh) Rafinesque

10–25 cm., terrestrial, glabrous; leaves five or six in whorl at top of greenish stem; inflorescence normally a solitary flower, sometimes two flowers from top of stem; sepals linear-oblong, about 20 mm. long, green, widely spread; petals oblanceolate, pale green, converging above lip; lip three-lobed, greenish white veined green, lateral lobes narrow, middle lobe rounded, slightly wavy, center with yellowish green ridge; column slender with terminal anther; ovary short, pedicellate, 15 mm. long.

Can be distinguished by its greenish stem, shorter sepals, leaves deflexed as bud opens, and flower pedicel only 5 mm. long. An extremely rare orchid found in a few scattered localities in Michigan, New York, Pennsylvania, Vermont, New Hampshire, Maine, Massachusetts, Connecticut, New Jersey, Virginia, North Carolina, and Missouri. Grows in open dry deciduous woodlands where plants grow in deep leaf litter. Flowers from mid-May in the south of its range to mid-June farther north. May lie dormant without flowering for several years.

Rose Pogonia *Pogonia*

The genus *Pogonia* as now understood consists of about three species, only one of which occurs in North America. Roots fibrous, slender; stem with single leaf and inflorescence of one to three bright pink flowers; sepals spreading but petals converging over the bearded lip; column free with hinged terminal anther.

Rose Pogonia *Pogonia ophioglossoides* (Linnaeus) Jussieu

8–35 cm., terrestrial; stem slender, green to purplish at base; leaf solitary, rarely two leaves, borne about halfway up stem; inflorescence one to three pink (sometimes white) terminal flowers; floral bract leaflike; sepals pink, elliptic, spreading, petals pink, somewhat broader than sepals, converging loosely over lip; lip spatulate, pink with fringed margin red, deeply fringed at apex; middle of lip with three rows of yellow bristles, wider and redder toward apex; column slender with hinged anther at end; ovary slender.

Can be recognized by its pink flowers and strongly bearded lip. Distribution in eastern North America from Ontario and Quebec east to Newfoundland, south to Florida, Alabama, Mississippi, Louisiana, and southeastern Texas. A local but not uncommon species growing in marshes, sphagnum bogs, wet meadows, and wet drainage ditches; sometimes in large colonies. Flowers from March in south of its range to August in Canada.

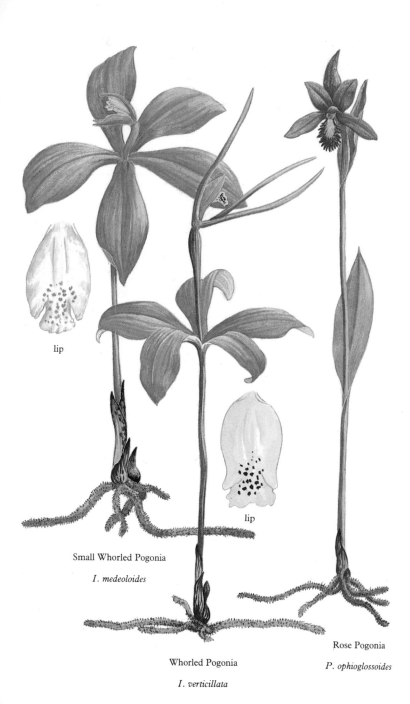

lip

Small Whorled Pogonia

I. medeoloides

lip

Whorled Pogonia

I. verticillata

Rose Pogonia

P. ophioglossoides

Vanilla Orchids *Vanilla*

A group of climbing plants, more or less branched; roots borne at the nodes, leafy or without leaves. Young plants terrestrial; mature plants lose contact with soil. Flowers large and fleshy with spreading sepals and petals. The vanilla of commerce, *V. planifolia,* is one of the five species recorded from Florida.

Link Vine *Vanilla barbellata* Reichenbach filius
Leafless vine; stem jointed producing bracts and aerial roots at the nodes; floral bracts short, 5–10 mm. long; sepals and petals yellowish green, spreading; lip three-lobed, margins involute, lateral lobes rounded, greenish below, deep rose-magenta above, shading to white at margin; column slightly curved with terminal anther; ovary cylindric, 50 mm. long.

Relatively common in hammocks of southern Florida. Can be distinguished by its lack of permanent leaves, yellowish sepals, and petals less than 5 cm. long, white margin at edge of lip, and middle lobe not longer than side lobes. Confined to southern Florida, growing in hammocks and in scrub over limestone rock. Flowers from June to July.

Dillon's Leafless Vanilla *Vanilla dilloniana* Correll
Leafless vine; similar to Link Vine in general appearance, but flower with longer and more slender sepals and petals, which are green rather than yellowish green; lip with middle lobe longer than laterals and magenta-red to margin.

Known in the United States from a single collection in Brickell Hammock in South Miami, Florida, in 1928. Flowers during May and June.

Link Vine

V. barbellata

Dillon's Leafless Vanilla

V. dilloniana

Leafy Vanilla *Vanilla phaeantha* Reichenbach filius
Leafy vine, stem green, rounded, climbing, branching; leaf and an aerial root borne from a node every 10–25 cm., leaves oblong, fleshy; inflorescence up to twelve large greenish flowers from side of a leaf axil; floral bract leaflike, up to 6 cm.; sepals and petals pale green, oblanceolate; lip tubular, obscurely three-lobed, apex truncate, white with fine yellow markings; column curved with terminal anther; ovary rounded, 8 cm. long.
Perhaps the most frequent Vanilla in Florida. Distinguished from *V. planifolia* by its flowers which are more than 7 cm. long. Known in the United States only from southern Florida where it grows in hammocks and wooded swamps. Flowers from May to July.

Vanilla *Vanilla planifolia* Andrews
Leafy vine, the producer of the vanilla bean of commerce; stem green, rounded, climbing, and branching; bearing a leaf and an aerial root from nodes 8–12 cm. apart; leaves single from each node, fleshy, oblong; inflorescence up to fifteen yellowish green flowers borne laterally from a leaf axil; flowers transient, lasting only twelve hours; floral bract green, triangular; sepals and petals pale yellowish green; lip tubular, striped yellow, obscurely three-lobed, margin fringed; column curved with terminal anther; ovary stout, rounded, 4 cm. long.
Distinguished from *V. phaeantha* by shorter flowers (less than 6 cm. long) and more deeply fringed lip. Known in the United States only from southern Florida; not uncommon in the Fahka-hatchee Swamp. Flowers during April.

Scentless Vanilla *Vanilla inodora* Schiede
Leafy vine; stem green, rounded, climbing, branching, a single leaf and aerial root from each node every 5–8 cm.; leaves broadly ovate, fleshy but relatively thin; inflorescence five to six green flowers with white lip; floral bract ovate, leaflike; sepals and petals oblong, lanceolate, green, with wavy margins; lip three-lobed, lateral lobes rounded surrounding the column, central lobe ovate with wavy margin, central fleshy yellow ridge; column slightly curved with terminal anther; ovary rounded, 45 mm. long.
First discovered growing in a hammock in southern Florida in 1953. Found several times since then but remains a rare species in the United States. A sporadic flowerer, blooms appearing from April to September.

Scentless Vanilla

V. inodora

Leafy Vanilla

V. phaeantha

Vanilla

V. planifolia

Dragon's Mouth *Arethusa*

A monotypic genus confined to northeastern North America. Characterized by bulbous corm and a solitary leaf that develops after the flower opens; inflorescence a solitary flower, rarely two, terminating the stem; sepals and petals subequal; lip crested; column adherent to lip, dilated above, resembling a petal.

Dragon's Mouth *Arethusa bulbosa* Linnaeus

6–40 cm., terrestrial, glabrous; leaf solitary, lanceolate, developing after flowering; inflorescence a solitary flower on top of stem, magenta to white; floral bract, scalelike; sepals erect, oblanceolate, laterals curved; petals curved above lip; lip indistinctly three-lobed, middle lobe curved downward with crenulate margins, yellow ridges down center, becoming fringed toward apex; column elongated with lateral wings, pink; ovary subsessile, erect, 15 mm. long.

Erect sepals, falcate petals, and crested lip are distinctive. Distribution from southern Ontario and Quebec east to Newfoundland; south through the Great Lakes area, east to Maine and Nova Scotia, south to Pennsylvania; also in mountains of North Carolina. Grows mainly in sphagnum bogs, marshes, and swamps, but also below rhododendrons at higher altitudes in North Carolina. Flowers from May in south of range to August in Canada.

Grass Pinks *Calopogon*

A small genus of four species, all of which are confined to eastern North America. Terrestrial with one or two grasslike leaves arising from a corm; flowers magenta, pink, or white with spreading sepals and petals in a terminal raceme of nonresupinate flowers (lip directed upward); lip strongly dilated with numerous clubbed hairs resembling stamens; column long and curved with pair of rounded wings near apex; anther terminal.

Bearded Grass Pink *Calopogon barbatus* (Walter) Ames

25–40 cm., terrestrial, glabrous; leaves one or two, very slender, erect; inflorescence in a loosely flowered raceme, three to five flowers, pink, opening in rapid succession; floral bracts ovate, half length of ovary; flowers nonresupinate with lip uppermost; sepals and petals spreading, pink; lip obscurely three-lobed, middle lobe dilated with bunch of orange stamenlike hairs in center; column slender, curved upward, winged toward apex; ovary slender, pedicellate, 10 mm. long.

Can be recognized by its relatively small flowers with dorsal sepal less than 20 mm. long, its lateral sepals spreading, not reflexed, and petals widest below the middle. A rather uncommon species recorded from North and South Carolina south to Florida, east to Louisiana. Grows in acid damp meadows, pine woodlands, grassy swamps, hammocks, more rarely in more open woodland. Flowers from February to May.

Many-Flowered Grass Pink *Calopogon multiflorus* Lindley

15–30 cm., terrestrial, glabrous; leaves one or two, linear, from dark green to purplish; inflorescence densely or laxly flowered, elongated, six to ten pink flowers opening in rapid succession; floral bracts ovate, shorter than ovary; sepals and petals spreading; petals widest above middle; lip directed upward, obscurely three-lobed with small rounded basal lobes, central lobe broadly dilated with cluster of bright orange stamenlike hairs; column slender, curved upward, winged at apex; ovary slender, pedicellate, 10 mm. long.

Differs from the closely related *C. barbatus* in having petals widest above the middle and inflorescence usually with more flowers. An uncommon species found in southern Georgia, Florida, and southern areas of Alabama and Mississippi. Grows in open marshy meadows, coniferous woodlands, and seepage areas. Flowers from March to July with a peak in April.

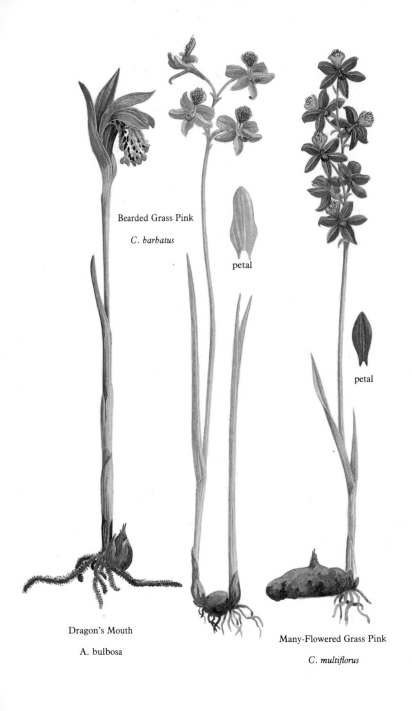

Bearded Grass Pink

C. barbatus

petal

petal

Dragon's Mouth

A. bulbosa

Many-Flowered Grass Pink

C. multiflorus

Pale Grass Pink *Calopogon pallidus* Chapman

20–50 cm., terrestrial; leaves one or two, narrow, ribbed; inflorescence a laxly flowered raceme of up to twelve pink to white flowers opening in slow succession; floral bract shorter than ovary; sepals and petals spreading, lateral sepals sometimes reflexed; lip pointing upward, obscurely three-lobed, middle lobe dilated, rounded, or triangular; cluster of yellow or orange stamenlike hairs in center; column curved upward, winged toward apex; ovary slender, pedicellate, 7 mm. long.

Can be recognized by short ovary and pedicel and flowers opening in slow succession. Distribution from Virginia and North Carolina to southern Florida and Gulf Coast to Louisiana. Grows in wet areas, marshy depressions in grassland, coniferous woodlands, bogs, rivers, and swamps. Flowers from March to July.

Grass Pink *Calopogon tuberosus* (Linnaeus) Britton, Sterns, and Poggenberg
(Syn. *Calopogon pulchellus* [Salisbury] R. Brown in Aiton)

45–120 cm., terrestrial, glabrous; leaves 1, rarely 2, strongly ribbed; inflorescence a terminal raceme of three to twenty-five deep pink to white flowers opening almost simultaneously; nonresupinate, lip uppermost; floral bracts shorter than ovary; sepals spreading; petals widest toward base; lip obscurely three-lobed, middle lobe widely dilated toward apex, patch of pale purple bristles with yellow-tipped white hairs behind; column slender, curved forward, winged at apex; ovary stout, pedicellate, to 10 mm. long.

Distinguished by large size of both plant and flowers; middle sepal more than 20 mm. long. The most widely ranging of the grass pinks. Occurs from southern Ontario, Quebec, and Newfoundland, south to Florida, east to Texas. Locally not uncommon, growing in marshy meadows, swamps, bogs, low-altitude coniferous woods, and in Florida on hammocks. Flowers from March in the South to August in southern Canada.

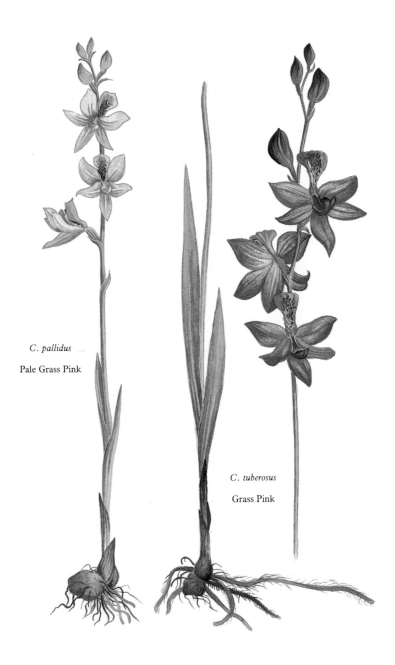

C. pallidus

Pale Grass Pink

C. tuberosus

Grass Pink

Small Prescotia *Prescotia*

Prescotia is a genus of tropical Central and South American orchids of which one species occurs in southern Florida. Characteristics include cluster of basal leaves; oval, fleshy roots; and a spike of numerous small flowers with the lip uppermost; sepals joined at base, forming a cup to which lip is also joined; column very small with dorsal anther.

Small Prescotia *Prescotia obligantha* (Swartz) Lindley
15–30 cm., terrestrial; leaves one to three, basal, stalked; inflorescence a spike of up to forty nonresupinate pinkish white flowers; floral bracts about as long as ovary; sepals ovate, recurving, laterals connate at base with base of lip; petals also recurved; lip uppermost, ovate, deeply concave; column very small; anther dorsal; ovary sessile, stout.
Identified by its basal leaves and flower spike with individual flowers less than 3 mm. long. In the United States known only from hammocks in southern Florida, growing in dense shade; rare. Flowers during February.

Jamaican Cranichis *Cranichis*

Another small genus of tropical terrestrial orchids of which one species has been recorded from Florida. Roots fleshy, leaves basal, stalked; stem sheathed by wide bracts. Raceme of small nonresupinate whitish flowers. Column small with lateral wings, apex toothed.

Jamaican Cranichis *Cranichis muscosa* Swartz
10–35 cm., terrestrial; leaves four or five in basal rosette, stalked; inflated bracts sheathing stem above leaves; inflorescence a terminal raceme of up to forty nonresupinate white flowers; floral bracts lanceolate, about same length as ovary; middle sepal recurved, lateral sepals spreading; petals linear-oblong; lip uppermost, suborbicular, concave; column 2 mm. long with lateral wings; ovary sessile, stout, 5 mm. long.
Distinguished by stalked basal leaf rosette and leaflike inflated bracts on stem; flowers less than 3 mm. long. Recorded from southern Florida over fifty years ago, but no recent records. Grows in shady hammocks. Flowers during January and February.

Shadow Witch *Ponthieva*

A group of terrestrial and epiphytic orchids found mainly in Central and South America; one species with one variety known from the United States. Characteristics include hairy roots, a basal leaf rosette, and an erect floral stem. Flowers white and green in lax terminal spiral, nonresupinate; sepals spreading; petals attached to column above base; lip uppermost, with concave center and pointed apex; column pointed; anther on dorsal surface.

Shadow Witch *Ponthieva racemosa* (Walter) Mohr
15–60 cm., terrestrial, partly pubescent; leaves three to eight, stalked, in basal rosette; stem with narrow bracts; inflorescence a terminal spiral of up to thirty horizontal or slightly ascending green and white flowers, lip uppermost; floral bracts lanceolate, shorter than ovary; middle sepal greenish with darker green veining, lateral sepals greenish with bright green veins; petals triangular, apices adherent with apex of middle sepal; lip white with green concave center and long pointed apex; column pointed with anther on dorsal surface; ovary stout, pedicellate, nearly horizontal or slightly ascending.
Differs from *Prescotia* and *Cranichis* in having flowers more than 3.5 mm. long, also in its spiral raceme and special lip structure. Ranges from Virginia south to Florida, west to southeast Texas. Grows in damp forests, springs, seepage areas, and banks of streams. Flowers from September in the northern part of its range to February in the south.
Var. *brittonae* (Ames) Luer is smaller, the petals narrower, and flowers acutely ascending; leaves fading or absent during time of flowering. Grows in open coniferous woodland on limestone. Known only from southern Florida. Flowers from December to February.

Small Prescotia

P. obligantha

Jamaican Cranichis

C. muscosa

Shadow Witch

P. racemosa

Ladies' Tresses *Spiranthes*

A large polymorphic genus of over 300 species widely dispersed throughout the temperate regions of the world. Many species are both complex and variable, and the status of some is still a matter of controversy. In most species the flowers are arranged spirally up the flower stalk. Other characteristics are their terrestrial habit; clustered tuberous or rarely fibrous roots; leaves variable, present or absent at time of flowering; flowers more or less tubular in appearance; lip toothed or three-lobed with erose margin; column short or elongate, footless or with a long foot at base; anther erect on back of column.

Nodding Ladies' Tresses *Spiranthes cernua* (Linnaeus) L. C. Richard
20–50 cm., terrestrial to semi-aquatic; leaves three to six, basal, linear-oblanceolate, green; inflorescence, a raceme of up to 60 flowers in more than one rank, white with yellowish centers, not conspicuously spiraled, flower spike cylindrical; floral bracts lanceolate, 5–15 mm. long; sepals white, lanceolate; petals similar, slightly falcate; lip white with pale greenish yellow center, ovate, center constricted, apex rounded or subacute, crenulate, recurved; column green, 4 mm. long with dorsal anther; ovary sessile, stout, 10 mm. long.
Can be recognized by relatively large flowers in more than one rank, flowers white with a yellowish green tinge in center, lip more than 9 mm. long, constricted near center. The similar *S. ochroleuca* has yellowish flowers. Distribution throughout the eastern half of the United States and Canada. Typical habitats include marshy fields and grasslands, wet woodlands, lakeshores, and wet roadside ditches. Flowers from September to November.

Fragrant Ladies' Tresses *Spiranthes odorata* (Nuttall) Lindley
30 cm.–1 m., semi-aquatic to aquatic, pubescent; leaves 3–6, linear-oblanceolate, borne on lower half of stem; inflorescence several vertical ranks of flowers, creamy white and very fragrant; floral bracts lanceolate, 15 mm. long; sepals lanceolate, lateral sepals oblique; petals similar, falcate; lip white with yellowish center, tapering to apex, crenulate, recurved, 14 mm. long; column 5 mm. long.
Very similar to *S. cernua*, but lip longer and not constricted near center, and the flowers are very fragrant. Southeastern in distribution, ranging from Virginia and North Carolina south to Florida, east to Texas. Habitats include wet woodlands, grassy alkaline marshes, and wet depressions in grassland; often grows in water. Flowers from October to March.

Narrow-Lipped Ladies' Tresses *Spiranthes cranichoides* (Grisebach) Cogniaux
20–40 cm., terrestrial; leaves 4–6, stalked, in basal rosette, green to reddish, ovate; inflorescence a slender stalk with bracts, pubescent above, purplish green with 10–30 greenish brown flowers in lax raceme; floral bracts lanceolate, 8 mm. long; dorsal sepal oblong-elliptic, dark greenish brown, lateral sepals lanceolate, light greenish brown; petals oblanceolate, pinkish; lip obscurely three-lobed with erect basal lamellae, lateral lobes broad, upcurved, pink, middle lobe broadly expanded, white; column 4 mm. long with dorsal anther; ovary sessile, stout.
A very distinctive species identified by its basal leaf rosette, nonspiraled flower spike, and shallow three-lobed lip expanded at apex; with large basal lamellae; *S. elata* has an entire lip, and *S. costaricensis* has apex of lip narrow. Distribution confined to Florida. Grows in damp, shady forests. Flowers in March.

Durango Ladies' Tresses *Spiranthes durangensis* Ames & Schweinfurth
20–40 cm., terrestrial, pubescent; leaves 2–3, linear-lanceolate, completely withered at flowering time; inflorescence, stem with tubular bracts; flower spike laxly flowered, up to 15 large, deflexed flowers, pinkish white with green veining; dorsal sepal ovate-lanceolate, concave, pale pink, lateral sepals linear-lanceolate, oblique; petals adherent to dorsal sepal, linear falciform; lip violin-shaped, constricted in middle, undulating, white with green veining; column flattened, 8 mm. long; anther dorsal; ovary stout, 10 mm. long.

Yellow Nodding
Ladies' Tresses
S. ochroleuca

Great Plains
Ladies' Tresses
S. magnicamporum

(Continued on next text page)

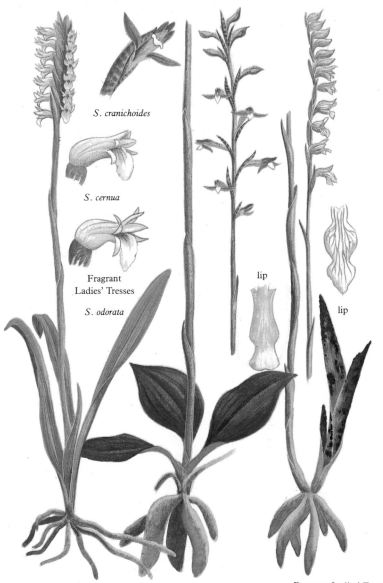

S. cranichoides

S. cernua

Fragrant
Ladies' Tresses

S. odorata

lip

lip

Nodding Ladies' Tresses

S. cernua

Narrow-Lipped Ladies' Tresses

S. cranichoides

Durango Ladies' Tresses

S. durangensis

Easily recognized by its green-veined, pinkish white nodding flowers. Mainly a Mexican species found in the U.S. only in the Chisos Mountains of southern Texas where it is rare. Grows in mountain grassland. Flowers from May to July.

Yellow Nodding Ladies' Tresses *Spiranthes ochroleuca* (Rydberg) Rydberg

20–50 cm., terrestrial, pubescent above, glabrous below; leaves 3–6, linear-oblanceolate, basal and on lower part of stem, extending up stem as leafy bracts; inflorescence up to 60 flowers in several ranks in single spiral; flowers pale yellowish; floral bracts lanceolate, 15 mm. long; sepals lanceolate; petals linear-lanceolate; lip broadly ovate, apex dilated, crenulate and with basal tuberosities, 10–11 mm. long; column 4 mm. long with dorsal anther; ovary sessile, stout.

Very similar to *S. cernua*, but flowers pale yellowish with large basal tuberosities toward base of lip. Northeastern distribution ranging from southwest Newfoundland south to Pennsylvania, west to the Great Lakes. Grows in shady woodlands and well-drained areas, not in marshes or wet grassland. Flowers during September and October.

Great Plains Ladies' Tresses *Spiranthes magnicamporum* Sheviak

10–50 cm., terrestrial, pubescent; leaves linear-lanceolate, absent at flowering time; a few leafy bracts on stem; inflorescence densely spiraled, flowers in several vertical rows, varying from white to cream-colored; floral bracts ovate, 10 mm. long; sepals linear-lanceolate; petals linear, adherent to dorsal sepal; lip entire, oblong-ovate, 7–11 mm. long; margin slightly serrate, apex reflexed, center yellowish, basal protuberances small; column 3 mm. long with dorsal anther; ovary sessile, 7 mm. long.

Very closely related to *S. cernua*, *S. ochroleuca*, and *S. odorata*. Best distinguished by its lack of leaves at flowering, its ovate lip not constricted in center, and its midwestern distribution. *S. odorata* has leaves on the stem and occurs in the southeast. *S. cernua* and *S. ochroleuca* have the lip constricted near the center. *S. magnicamporum* ranges from North Dakota and Minnesota south to Texas, east to Illinois, Indiana, and Ohio; also Alabama, Colorado, Utah, and New Mexico. Grows on calcareous grasslands in dry situations. Flowers from mid-September to November.

Tall Neottia *Spiranthes elata* (Swartz) L. C. Richard

25–50 cm., terrestrial; leaves six–seven, elliptic with long stalks in an erect basal rosette; inflorescence a slender stem with bracts, pubescent above, purplish green, with laxly flowered raceme of ten to thirty greenish brown tubular flowers; floral bracts lanceolate, longer than ovary; dorsal sepal lanceolate, yellowish brown, lateral sepals linear-oblong, buff-brown; petals spatulate, pale brown with dark stripe down center; lip entire, ovate with erect basal lamellae, base concave, green, lip narrowed in middle and broadly expanded at apex, which is white, 5 mm. long; column 2 mm. long, dorsal anther; ovary sessile, stout, 7 mm. long.

Can be identified by its unspiraled flower spike, basal rosette of long-stalked leaves, entire lip, and much expanded lip apex. Distribution confined to southern Florida where it is most uncommon, growing in shady hammocks. Flowers during March.

Costa Rican Ladies' Tresses *Spiranthes costaricensis* Reichenbach filius

20–30 cm., terrestrial; leaves four or five, elliptic, with long stems in basal rosette, withering as plant flowers; inflorescence a slender stem with bracts, pubescent above, green, laxly flowered spike of ten to thirty-five white flowers with green markings; floral bracts lanceolate, 12 mm. long; dorsal sepal obovate, white with green stripe, lateral sepals oblanceolate with similar coloring; petals obovate, falcate, white with green stripe; lip three-lobed with erect basal lamellae, lateral lobes rounded, central lobe with apex narrow, white with central green stripe, lip 4.5 mm. long; column 2 mm. long with dorsal anther; ovary sessile, stout.

Easily distinguished by its long-stemmed leaf rosette, which withers at flowering, and its white, green-striped flower parts. A very rare species in the United States, known only from Everglades National Park where it grows in wooded hammocks. Flowers during March and April.

(Continued on next text page)

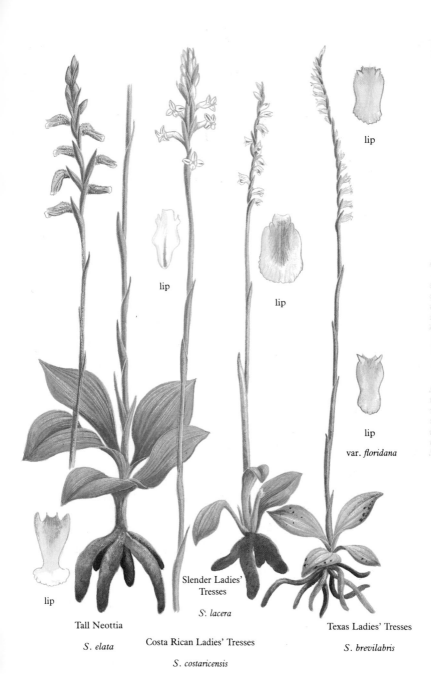

lip

lip

lip

lip

lip
var. *floridana*

lip

Slender Ladies'
Tresses

S. lacera

lip

Tall Neottia

S. elata

Costa Rican Ladies' Tresses

S. costaricensis

Texas Ladies' Tresses

S. brevilabris

Slender Ladies' Tresses *Spiranthes lacera* (Rafinesque) Rafinesque

25–50 cm., terrestrial, pubescent; leaves three to five, ovate with stems in basal rosette, commonly persisting during flowering; inflorescence an elongated spike of up to forty white flowers with green centers, laxly spiraled or flowers in a row on one side of stem; floral bracts ovate, 6 mm. long; sepals elliptic; petals linear, oblique; lip entire, oblong, white with green center, margin of apex slightly serrate; column 2 mm. long; anther dorsal; ovary sessile, stout.

Distributed mainly in the Northeast, east to Manitoba, south to Tennessee. Grows in grasslands and open woodlands. Flowers from June to August.

Var. *gracilis* (Bigelow) Luer is usually a very slender plant, and its basal rosette of leaves is gone by flowering time; its flower spike is well spiraled. Most frequent in the Southwest where it flowers from September to November.

Texas Ladies' Tresses *Spiranthes brevilabris* Lindley

20–40 cm., terrestrial, densely pubescent; leaves three to five, ovate with short stalks in basal rosette; inflorescence a slender stem with bracts; flower spike of a single rank of flowers, secund or spiraled; flowers yellowish white; flower bracts ovate, 6 mm. long; sepals and petals elliptic, yellowish white; lip entire with basal protuberances, center yellow, apex dilated with undulate, serrated margin; column green, 1.5 mm. long; anther dorsal; ovary sessile, stout.

Distinguished by basal ovate leaves often withering at flowering, dense pubescence, and yellow-centered lip. Distribution in the United States occurs in northern Florida, southern Georgia, west to southeastern Texas. Grows in dry pastures, coniferous woods, and sandy areas. Flowers from February to May.

Var. *floridana* (Wherry) Luer has a more extensive range, north to North Carolina; differs mainly in lacking the dense pubescence of the typical plant.

Little Ladies' Tresses *Spiranthes tuberosa* Rafinesque

(Syn. *Spiranthes grayi* Ames)

(Syn. *Spiranthes simplex* A. Gray)

10–30 cm., terrestrial, glabrous; root an elongated tuber; leaves two or three, basal, stalked, ovate, not present at flowering; inflorescence very slender with tiny bracts along stem; flowers white, in a single rank, spiraled, or secund; floral bracts lanceolate, 2–5 mm. long; sepals lanceolate; petals similar, slightly oblique; lip entire, ovate with two basal protuberances, undulate, slightly serrated margin; column green, 1.5 mm. long; anther dorsal; ovary sessile, very small.

Distinguished by its very slender habit, its root an elongated tuber, its small white flowers, and its lack of leaves at flowering time. Eastern and southeastern in distribution; ranges from Massachusetts south to Florida, west to Illinois and Missouri, southwest to eastern Texas. Grows in grasslands and open woodlands. Flowers from June in the south of its range to October in the North.

Lace-Lipped Spiral Orchid *Spiranthes laciniata* (Small) Ames

20–60 cm., terrestrial, pubescent; leaves four or five, linear-lanceolate, keeled, basal to lower part of stem; inflorescence a stout or slender stem with bracts, raceme of up to fifty whitish or yellow flowers arranged in a single line, either spiraled or secund; floral bracts lanceolate, 12 mm. long; sepals lanceolate, white; petals linear, curved, white; lip entire, ovate, white with yellow center, crenulate margin, basal protuberances incurved; column green, 2 mm. long; anther dorsal, ovary sessile, stout, 5 mm. long.

Very similar to *S. vernalis*, their main difference being the incurved basal lip protuberances in *S. laciniata*. Distribution from New Jersey south through the Atlantic states to Florida, west to southeastern Texas. Favors as a habitat damp grasslands, seepages, and woodlands. Flowers from April in the south of its range to August in the north.

(Continued on next text page)

lip

lip

lip

lip

tle Ladies' Tresses

S. tuberosa

Lace-Lipped Spiral Orchid

S. laciniata

Wide-Leaved Ladies' Tresses

S. lucida

Giant Spiral Orchid

S. longilabris

Giant Spiral Orchid *Spiranthes longilabris* Lindley

30–50 cm., terrestrial, sparsely pubescent, leaves three to five, basal, linear-lanceolate, keeled, often absent at time of flowering; inflorescence a variable stem, slender or stout, with bracts, spike of up to thirty white flowers with a yellow center, in a single line, secund or slightly spiraled; floral bracts lanceolate, 10 mm. long; sepals white, lanceolate, lateral sepals widely spread; petals white, lanceolate, slightly curved; lip entire, ovate with yellow center; erect basal protuberances, apex crenulate, recurved, 9 mm. long; column green, 2 mm. long with dorsal anther; ovary sessile, stout, 7 mm. long.

Can be recognized by its flowers in one rank, secund or loosely spiraled; leaves, when present, narrow; lip with a yellow center; flowering late in the year. *S. laciniata*, which also has a yellow center, flowers in the spring. Distribution southeastern, from Virginia and North Carolina south to Florida, west to eastern Texas. Occurs in damp coniferous woods and wet grasslands. Flowers in November and December.

Wide-Leaved Ladies' Tresses *Spiranthes lucida* (H. H. Elton) Ames

20–35 cm., terrestrial, glabrous below to sparsely pubescent above; leaves three or four, basal and enveloping the lower stem, elliptic to lanceolate; inflorescence a slender stem with only a few bracts, raceme usually in three ranks, generally spiraled; flowers up to twenty, white with bright yellow centers; floral bracts lanceolate, 10 mm. long; dorsal sepal linear, lateral sepals linear oblong; petals linear, rounded at apex; lip entire, oblong with margin rounded and crenulate, basal protuberances present; column white, 3 mm. long with dorsal anther; ovary sessile, stout, 5 mm. long.

Best distinguished by its bright yellow center, northeastern distribution and early flowering. Ranges from Nova Scotia south to Pennsylvania, west to Michigan and Illinois; also Missouri, Kansas, and Wisconsin. Fairly common but local, growing along lake margins, in damp meadows and on sandbars in rivers and streams. Flowers from May to August.

Michoacán Ladies' Tresses *Spiranthes michuacana* (Lexarza) Hemsley

20–40 cm., terrestrial, pubescent above, glabrous below, leaves three to five, linear-lanceolate in a basal rosette and on lower part of stem, withered by flowering time; inflorescence a stout stem with sheathing bracts, raceme not conspicuously spiraled; flowers twenty-five to thirty, white with green stripes and pubescent margins; floral bracts ovate, 25 mm. long; dorsal sepal linear-ovate, lateral sepals linear-oblong; petals linear, falcate; lip entire, ovate, tapering toward apex, white with fine green markings, 15 mm. long, basal protuberances small, pubescent; column stout, 6 mm. long; ovary stout, hairy, 10 mm. long.

Distinguished from related *S. durangensis* by smaller flowers and lip without central constriction. A Mexican species that has been recorded a few times from mountains of southern Arizona and southwestern Texas. Grows on grassy mountain slopes. Flowers from September to February.

Oval Ladies' Tresses *Spiranthes ovalis* Lindley

20–40 cm., terrestrial, pubescent; leaves two or three, oblanceolate, basal, and sheathing lower portion of stem; a few bracts above; inflorescence slender with narrow raceme of up to fifty white flowers, spiraled weakly; floral bracts ovate, 8 mm. long; sepals white, lanceolate; petals similar; lip entire, ovate, white, with basal protuberances, apex expanded, recurved, 5 mm. long; column green, 2 mm. long with dorsal anther; ovary sessile, stout, 6 mm. long.

Distinguished by its small white flowers without a colored center, its two or three basal leaves, its autumn flowering, and its southeastern range. Distribution from Virginia west to Missouri, south to Florida and Texas, growing in the shade of damp woodlands. Flowers from September to November.

Red-Spot Ladies' Tresses *Spiranthes parasitica* A. Richard and Galeotti

15–30 cm., terrestrial, sparsely pubescent; leaves five or six, ovate, stalked, in a basal rosette, disintegrate by flowering time; inflorescence a slender stem with few bracts; raceme of up to twelve white flowers, spiraled; floral bracts lanceolate, translucent, 10 mm. long; dorsal sepal oblong, lateral sepals similar but oblique; petals spatulate; lip entire, oblong with ill-defined protuberances

(Continued on next text page)

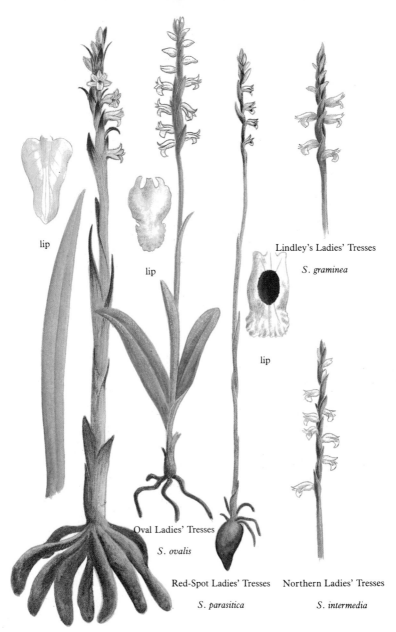

lip

lip

lip

Lindley's Ladies' Tresses

S. graminea

lip

Oval Ladies' Tresses

S. ovalis

Red-Spot Ladies' Tresses

S. parasitica

Northern Ladies' Tresses

S. intermedia

Michoacán Ladies' Tresses

S. michuacana

at base, constricted above center, apex expanded and crenulate with three thin green lines, center of lip concave with a distinctive red patch; column green, 3 mm. long with dorsal anther; ovary pubescent, 5 mm. long.

Similar to *S. elata*, but distinguished from that species and all others by the red lip patch. Mainly Mexican species that turns up from time to time on grassy mountain slopes and in coniferous forests in Arizona, New Mexico, and southwestern Texas. Flowers during June and July.

Lindley's Ladies' Tresses *Spiranthes graminea* Lindley

25–50 cm., terrestrial, pubescent above; leaves two to four, linear-oblanceolate, basal and on lower section of stem; bracts above; inflorescence a spiraled spike of up to forty small white flowers, often arranged in four vertical lines, pubescent; floral bracts ovate, 9 mm. long; dorsal sepals lanceolate; petals oblong-lanceolate; lip oblong with large basal protuberances, apex truncate, undulate, 7.5 mm. long; column 3 mm. long with dorsal anther; ovary subsessile, stout, 5 mm. long.

Can be recognized by its all-white flowers, oblong, truncate lip and distribution. Mexican species, which was discovered in 1968 in southern Arizona. Grows in wet grasslands. Flowers from June to September.

Northern Ladies' Tresses *Spiranthes intermedia* Ames

20–40 cm., terrestrial, pubescent; leaves two to four, linear-lanceolate, stalked, basal; stem with bracts above leaves; inflorescence stout or slender with spike of up to thirty creamy white flowers, spiraled, frequently in two or more vertical lines; floral bracts ovate-lanceolate, 12 mm. long; sepals lanceolate, lateral sepals spreading slightly; petals oblong; lip ovate with a pale yellow center, basal protuberances short, apex slightly serrated; column 2 mm. long with dorsal anther; ovary sessile, stout, 6 mm. long.

Similar to *S. vernalis*, but flower spike more spiraled and flowers cream-colored. *S. porrifolia* has lateral sepals appressed to other floral parts, not free as in *S. intermedia*, and is western in range, not northeastern. *S. intermedia* is an uncommon, local species found in the northeast from extreme southern Ontario and Quebec to Maine and Connecticut. Grows in open grasslands. Flowers from August to September.

Green Ladies' Tresses *Spiranthes polyantha* Reichenbach filius

15–30 cm., terrestrial, slightly pubescent; leaves one to three, basal, elliptic, short-stalked, not present at flowering time; inflorescence a slender stem with bracts, purplish green; laxly flowered with ten to forty small greenish brown flowers, tubular with tips of floral segments recurved; floral bracts lanceolate, 6 mm. long; dorsal sepal oblanceolate, reddish green; lateral sepals linear-oblanceolate, grayish green; petals oblanceolate, curved, grayish with pink tinge; lip elliptic narrowing to apex, recurved, grayish green, tinted pink, lateral sepals and lip expanded to form a small mentum; column 1 mm. long with dorsal anther; ovary sessile, stout, 6 mm. long.

Easily recognized by its color, its tubular form, its recurved sepals, and its slender lip. In the United States known only from Florida, where it grows in dry woodlands on rocky soil. Flowers during February and March.

Grass-Leaved Ladies' Tresses *Spiranthes praecox* (Walter) S. Watson

20–60 cm., terrestrial, pubescent; leaves five or six, linear-lanceolate, keeled and rigid, basal; inflorescence a variable stem with bracts, with spike of twenty to forty white flowers with green-veined lips; spiral variable; floral bracts lanceolate, 10 mm. long; sepals lanceolate; petals linear, curved; lip oblong, white with green veins, pubescent basal protuberances, apex expanded, crenulate; column green, 2 mm. long with dorsal anther; ovary sessile, stout, 5 mm. long.

Best identified by short green veins on lip. Distribution southeastern, from New Jersey south to Florida, west to eastern Texas. Grows in wet grassland, woodlands, and roadside ditches. Flowers from February to June.

(Continued on next text page)

Leek-Leaved Ladies' Tresses

S. porrifolia

Grass-Leaved Ladies' Tresses

S. praecox

Green Ladies' Tresses

S. polyantha

Hooded Ladies' Tresses

S. romanzoffiana

Rush-Leaved Ladies' Tresses

S. tortilis

Hooded Ladies' Tresses *Spiranthes romanzoffiana* Chamisso
20–50 cm., terrestrial, pubescent above, glabrous below; leaves three to six, linear-lanceolate, mainly basal, extending up stem as bracts; inflorescence a crowded spike with up to sixty creamy white flowers in three vertical ranks; floral bracts lanceolate, 20 mm. long; dorsal sepal lanceolate, lateral sepals similar but curved; petals linear; lip violin-shaped, constricted above middle, apex finely serrate, recurved; column 2 mm. long with dorsal anther; ovary sessile, stout, 8 mm. long. Differs from the similar *S. porrifolia* in shape of lip, which in *S. porrifolia* is ovate with the apex not dilated. *S. romanzoffiana* is a common species in the North, ranging from Alaska across Canada and the northern United States to Newfoundland; in the West it occurs south to California, Arizona, and New Mexico. Grows in a variety of habitats: tundra, bogs, open woodlands, and littoral areas. Flowers from July to October.

Leek-Leaved Ladies' Tresses *Spiranthes porrifolia* Lindley
20–50 cm., terrestrial, glabrous; leaves three to five, elliptic-lanceolate, basal or on lower portion of stem, sometimes absent at flowering time; stem with a few bracts above leaves; inflorescence a dense spiral of up to forty small yellowish flowers in several vertical ranks; floral bracts lanceolate, 12 mm. long; dorsal sepal lanceolate, lateral sepals similar but oblique; petals linear-lanceolate; lip ovate, not expanded at apex, base with prominent protuberances; column 2 mm. long with dorsal anther; ovary sessile, stout, 2.5 mm. long.
Similar to *S. romanzoffiana*, but lip ovate and not expanded at apex. Western in distribution, from southern Washington to southern California. Grows on seepage slopes, along streams, and in bogs in the mountains. Flowers from May to August.

Rush-Leaved Ladies' Tresses *Spiranthes tortilis* (Swartz) L. C. Richard
20–50 cm., terrestrial, slightly pubescent; leaves two or three, long and slender, often withering at flowering; stem with bracts above leaves; inflorescence slender, with a spike of up to sixty small white flowers with green centers, spiraled or secund; floral bracts ovate, 4 mm. long; sepals elliptic, white; petals elliptic, green and white; lip green with a white apex, ovate, apex rounded, crenulate; column green, 1 mm. long with dorsal anther; ovary sessile, stout, 3 mm. long.
Best distinguished by green center to lip. In the United States found only in southern Florida and the Florida Keys where it grows in rocky pinelands and among grass and palms. Flowers during May and June.

Spring Ladies' Tresses *Spiranthes vernalis* Engelmann and Gray   ·
20–60 cm., terrestrial, pubescent with hairs pointed, not clubbed; leaves four or five, linear-lanceolate, keeled and rigid, basal and enveloping lower portion of stem; stem with bracts above leaves; inflorescence a variable stem, spike of up to fifty whitish flowers with yellow centers, spiraled or secund; floral bracts lanceolate, 15 mm. long; sepals lanceolate; petals oblong; lip ovate, white with a yellow center, with erect basal protuberances, apex rounded, crenulate; column green, 2 mm. long with dorsal anther; ovary sessile, stout, 8 mm. long.
Can be identified by its narrow linear leaves, sharply pointed pubescent hairs, and yellow center of lip. Eastern and southeastern distribution from New Hampshire and Vermont south through Atlantic states to Florida, west to Texas and New Mexico, northwest to Nebraska, Kansas, and Oklahoma. A common species that grows in grassland, along road margins, and in other open areas. Flowers from February in the south of its range to August in the north.

Scarlet Ladies' Tresses *Spiranthes cinnabarina* (Lexarza) Hemsley
(Syn. *Stenorrhynchus cinnabarina* [Lexarza] Lindley)
30–50 cm., terrestrial, pubescent above, glabrous below; leaves three or four, linear-oblanceolate, ascending the stem; inflorescence a dense spike of thirty to forty vermilion to orange-red flowers with flower parts strongly recurved; floral bracts lanceolate, red, 35 mm. long; dorsal sepal lanceolate, lateral sepals lanceolate, oblique; petals linear, curved; lip lanceolate, yellow with vermilion apex; column 9 mm. long with dorsal anther; ovary stout, pubescent, 10 mm. long.

(Continued on next text page)

Scarlet Ladies' Tresses

S. cinnabarina

Leafless Beaked Orchid

S. lanceolata

Spring Ladies' Tresses

S. vernalis

Distinguished from *S. lanceolata* by presence of leaves at flowering time and by its recurved flower parts. A Mexican and Central American orchid recorded infrequently in the Chisos Mountains of Big Bend National Park in southern Texas where it grows on mountain slopes, in open woodland, and along creeks. Flowers from July to October.

Leafless Beaked Orchid *Spiranthes lanceolata* Reichenbach filius
(Syn. *Stenorrhynchus orchioides* [Swartz] L. C. Richard)
30–60 cm. terrestrial, pubescent; leaves four to six, oblong-elliptic, basal, absent at flowering time; inflorescence a stout stem with bracts; flower spike densely flowered with up to forty tubular coral red flowers; floral bracts lanceolate, red-brown, 18 mm. long; dorsal sepal lanceolate, lateral sepals lanceolate, oblique; petals lanceolate, curved, pale rose-red; lip from white to pink, lanceolate, the apex slightly recurved; column 14 mm. long; ovary stalked, stout.
Distinguished from *S. cinnabarina* by absence of leaves at flowering time and by the floral parts which are not so reflexed. Occurs in the United States only in Florida and the Florida Keys, growing in grassland and other open areas, in dry woodland, and along road verges. Flowers from April to July.
Var. *paludicola* Luer has brighter red flowers, and leaves persist during flowering. Grows in the Fahkahatchee Swamp. Flowers from January to March.
Var. *luteoalba* (Reichenbach filius) Luer is similar to the typical plant except that its flowers are green, not red. Very local in Florida, flowering during April.

Spurred Neottia *Centrogenium*

A small genus of about ten tropical American species of which one occurs in southern Florida. Characteristics include tuberous roots, long-stemmed leaves, and a laxly flowered spike; lateral sepals united with column foot to form a long spur to which the base of the lip is attached; column short, terminated by a pointed rostellum; dorsal anther.

Spurred Neottia *Centrogenium setaceum* (Lindley) Schlechter
30–50 cm., terrestrial, pubescent; roots tuberous, in a cluster; leaves one or two, basal, elliptic on long stalk; stalk slender, partly enveloped by leaf sheaths; inflorescence laxly flowered with three to ten greenish white flowers with lateral sepals widely spreading; floral bracts lanceolate, 24 mm. long; dorsal sepal lanceolate, concave, lateral sepals lanceolate, spreading, united at bases with column foot, enclosing base of the lip to form a spur; petals lanceolate, curved; lip linear, notched about middle and then ovate, shallowly fringed, recurved; column short with elongated foot and dorsal anther; ovary pedicellate, stout, 25 mm. long.
Easily recognized by its long-stalked leaf, spur, and lanceolate flower parts. In the United States known only from southern Florida. Grows in shady, moist hammocks. Flowers from January to March.

Rattlesnake Plantains *Goodyera*

A group of about twenty-five species with a worldwide distribution. Four species occur in North America. Characteristics are a horizontal creeping rhizome with roots at intervals and at its end a rosette of evergreen leaves with or without silvery white reticulations. Flowering stem rises from the rosette; often grows in colonies; sepals and petals connivent over column; lip with a beak-shaped apex; hybridization frequent when the ranges of two or more species overlap.

Menzies' Rattlesnake Plantain *Goodyera oblongifolia* Rafinesque
20–45 cm., terrestrial, densely pubescent; leaves three to seven, oblong-elliptic, dark green with whitish stripe down center of leaf, the remainder often reticulated; leaves form basal rosette with stem rising from center with a few bracts; inflorescence variable, spike densely or loosely flowered,

(Continued on next text page)

Menzies' Rattlesnake Plantain

Spurred Neottia

G. oblongifolia

Downy Rattlesnake Plantain

C. setaceum

G. pubescens

ten to thirty whitish flowers with green center; floral bracts lanceolate, 6–13 mm. long; dorsal sepal lanceolate, blunt, pale green, lateral sepals ovate, whitish with green center; petals spatulate, connivent with dorsal sepal over column, white with green vein; lip bulbous-saccate, white, with apex tonguelike, rounded, recurved; column short with pointed rostellum and dorsal anther; ovary subsessile, stout, 9 mm. long.

Can be recognized by floral parts more than 5 mm. long and leaves having a white center stripe. A mainly western species ranging from southern Alaska and British Columbia south to California, east to Great Lakes, north to southern Quebec, New Brunswick, and Maine; also in south central states and Arizona. A locally common species growing in both hardwood and coniferous forests, at low altitudes in the North, in the mountains in the South. Flowers from late July to September.

Downy Rattlesnake Plantain *Goodyera pubescens* (Willdenow) R. Brown in Aiton

25–50 cm., terrestrial, densely pubescent; leaves three to eight, oblong-elliptic, bluish green with prominent white reticulations, forming a basal rosette; flowering stem with a few bracts; inflorescence a densely flowered cylindrical spike of up to eighty white and greenish flowers; floral bract lanceolate, 5–9 mm. long; sepals ovate with narrowed apex, white with green vein; petals connivent with dorsal sepal over column; lip scrotiform, apex short and recurved, white; column short with blunt rostellum and terminal anther; ovary subsessile, stout, 5 mm. long.

Can be recognized by its cylindrical, densely flowered spike, broadly globose lip, and blunt rostellum. Ranges through the northeastern states south to Alabama, Georgia, and South Carolina. A locally common species, often forming large colonies. Grows largely in mountainous areas, in woodlands and thickets. Flowers from May to October with a peak in July and August.

Lesser Rattlesnake Plantain *Goodyera repens* (Linnaeus) R. Brown in Aiton

10–25 cm., terrestrial; leaves three to seven, ovate, dark green, sometimes reticulated with white veins, in basal rosette; stem rising from center with a few bracts; inflorescence a laxly flowered, one-sided spike of up to twenty white flowers; floral bracts lanceolate, 5–9 mm. long; sepals ovate, concave, lateral sepals oblique; petals oblong-spatulate, connivent with dorsal sepal over column; lip broadly globose-saccate, white or pinkish with pointed apex; column short with short rostellum and dorsal anther; ovary subsessile, stout, 7 mm. long.

Distinguished by its small size and broadly globose lip with short apex. *G. tesselata* has a narrower lip with a longer apex. A locally common species in the North, ranging from Alaska across Canada and the northern United States to Newfoundland, south locally to Arizona, New Mexico, and Tennessee. Grows in damp humus of coniferous forests, tundra, wooded areas, and thickets. Flowers during July and August.

Var. *ophioides* Fernald is the name given to the form with white reticulated leaves. Probably more common in North America than the typical form with all-green leaves.

Tessellated Rattlesnake Plantain *Goodyera tesselata* Loddiges

20–35 cm., terrestrial, densely pubescent; leaves three to eight, elliptic-lanceolate, bluish green with white reticulations, forming a basal rosette; stem from center of rosette with a few bracts; inflorescence a densely or sparsely flowered spike, one-sided or sometimes cylindrical, from five to forty white flowers; dorsal sepal oblong-lanceolate, lateral sepals ovate-lanceolate; petals spatulate, connivent with dorsal sepal over column; lip bulbous, relatively narrow, with pointed apex 2 mm. long; column short with pointed rostellum and dorsal anther; ovary subsessile, stout, 8 mm. long. Distinguished from *G. pubescens* by its narrowly saccate lip with a longer apex. Distribution northeastern, from the Great Lakes to Newfoundland, south to Pennsylvania and northern Virginia. Grows in both hardwood and coniferous forests, in drier situations than *G. repens*. Flowers during July and August.

(Continued on next text page)

Leaf of var.

ophioides

Tessellated Rattlesnake Plantain

G. tesselata

Low Erythrodes

E. querceticola

Lesser Rattlesnake Plantain

G. repens

Erythrodes *Erythrodes*

A group of about a hundred terrestrial and semi-epiphytic species with one species in the southeastern United States. Root system a creeping rhizome producing erect or ascending stems; leaves often reticulated, and some tropical species have beautiful variegated foliage; inflorescence a terminal raceme; flowers with dorsal sepal and petals forming a hood, lateral sepals free; lip with bulbous spur; column short with dorsal anther.

Low Erythrodes *Erythrodes querceticola* (Lindley) Ames

20–30 cm., terrestrial, ascending leafy stem from creeping rhizome; leaves three to eight, ovate to lanceolate, greenish, at intervals up the stem; inflorescence a densely or laxly flowered raceme of small yellowish white flowers; floral bracts ovate, 5 mm. long; dorsal sepal elliptic, concave, lateral sepals similar; petals lanceolate, connivent with dorsal sepal; lip with base elongated into a short, rounded spur, three-lobed, lateral lobes expanded and rounded, median lobe pointed and recurved; column short, 2 mm. long with dorsal anther; ovary sessile, stout, 5 mm. long.

Similar to the genus *Goodyera*, but distinguished by lip characteristics. In the United States occurs locally in Florida, Mississippi, Louisiana, and eastern Texas. Grows in moist woodlands and near springs and creeks. Flowers throughout the year in southern Florida, during July and August elsewhere.

Zeuxine Orchid *Zeuxine*

A genus of Old World orchids, one species of which has found its way to Florida, where it has become naturalized. Grasslike leaves overlapping and sheathing the stem; small creamy white flowers with yellow expanded lip. Grows in wet situations such as swamps and seepage areas, sometimes appearing even in grass lawns.

Zeuxine Orchid *Zeuxine strateumatica* (Linnaeus) Schlechter

15–25 cm., terrestrial with ascending leafy stems, succulent; leaves five to twelve, linear-lanceolate, keeled, overlapping up stem; inflorescence a densely flowered spike of eight to fifty white and yellow flowers; floral bracts lanceolate, 15 mm. long; dorsal sepal ovate, concave; lateral sepals ovate, oblique; petals ovate, curved, converging with dorsal sepal to form hood; lip adnate to base of column, narrow in middle, broadly expanded and rounded at apex, bright yellow; column short, 1.5 mm. long with dorsal anther; ovary sessile, stout.

Introduced into the United States, where it is now naturalized in Florida. Grows generally in wet habitats, such as swamps, marshes, and drainage ditches, but sometimes appears in lawns. Flowers during December and January.

Branched Orchid *Tropidia*

A small genus that occurs mainly in eastern Asia, with one species in the American tropics and West Indies ranging north into southern Florida. Root system a short rhizome and fibrous roots; strongly pleated leaves; inflorescence a compound raceme of numerous small greenish white flowers; sepals and petals spreading; lip entire and concave; column short with a dorsal anther.

Branched Orchid *Tropidia polystachya* (Swartz) Ames

25–35 cm., terrestrial, erect and branching; stem slender, jointed, branching; leaves one to five, alternate on stem, elliptic-lanceolate, strongly veined and pleated; inflorescence a branched raceme with ten to sixty greenish white widely spreading flowers; floral bracts lanceolate, 4 mm. long; sepals elliptic, lateral sepals curved; petals lanceolate, oblique; lip entire, concave, constricted in middle, apex expanded and notched, raised yellow patch toward base of lip; column short, 3 mm. long with dorsal anther; ovary sessile, slender, 8 mm. long.

In the United States known only from Florida where it grows in wooded limestone hammocks near Miami; now very rare. Flowers from September to November with a peak in October.

(*Continued on next text page*)

Zeuxine Orchid

Z. strateumatica

Branched Orchid

T. polystachya

Frosted Pleurothallis

P. gelida

Frosted Pleurothallis *Pleurothallis*

A large genus found in the American tropics, with one species recorded from southern Florida. Single-leaved stem; often growing in clumps; raceme of more or less pendent flowers; sepals usually connate at their bases; lip entire or three-lobed, attached to base of column, shorter than petals; column with or without a column foot; anther terminal.

Frosted Pleurothallis *Pleurothallis gelida* Lindley
10–45 cm., epiphytic; growing in clumps; solitary leaf, oblong-elliptic, terminating a stem with several tuberous sheaths; inflorescence a stalk from a sheath at leaf axil with a slender raceme of five to twenty-five yellowish white pubescent flowers, more or less pendent; floral bracts triangular, 1 mm. long; dorsal sepal ovate, concave, lateral sepals elliptic, fused at base; petals oblong with dentate apex; lip small, shallowly three-lobed, rectangular, attached to the column foot; column 2.5 mm. long; anther terminal; ovary slender on a short, curved pedicel, 2.5 mm. long.
Best identified by its resemblance to the lily of the valley. In the United States known only from the humid forest areas of southern Florida, where it grows in clusters on tree trunks and branches. Flowers from December to April.

Crimson Pygmy Orchid *Lepanthopsis*

Small genus of half a dozen miniature tropical American epiphytic orchids, one of which occurs in southern Florida. Very short erect stems encased in tubular sheaths with single terminal leaf; minute flowers in a raceme rising from within the uppermost sheath; sepals ovate, laterals partially connate behind lip; column very short with terminal anther.

Crimson Pygmy Orchid *Lepanthopsis melanantha* (Reichenbach filius) Ames
4–6 cm., epiphytic; stem from creeping rhizome, erect, concealed by enveloping tubular sheaths; leaf terminal, elliptic, from within uppermost sheath; inflorescence a very slender peduncle with a loose raceme of 5–7 minute carmine red flowers; floral bracts triangular, minute; sepals ovate, laterals connate to half their length, behind lip; petals orbicular; lip orbicular, fleshy with indistinct lateral lobes half surrounding column; column minute with terminal triangular anther; ovary on curved stalk, thick, 1 mm. long.
Easily recognized by minute size and carmine flowers. Known only from swamps in southern Florida. Grows either high in trees or relatively low on branches. Flowers may be found at any time of the year.

Snake's-Head Orchid *Restrepiella*

Another small genus of tropical American epiphytic orchids with one representative in southern Florida. Slender stem with enveloping bracts bearing a single leaf; flowers borne on short stalks near base of leaf; lateral sepals connate to apex; petals much shorter than sepals; lip attached to column foot; column with a terminal anther with 4 pollinia.

Snake's-Head Orchid *Restrepiella ophiocephala* (Lindley) Garay & Dunsterville
10–30 cm., epiphytic, stems and leaves growing in clusters; stem slender with tubular bracts; leaf solitary, oblong-lanceolate, terminal, with grooved stem 1–2 cm. long; inflorescence 1–3 subsessile yellowish flowers from apex of stem; floral parts fleshy, pubescent along margins; floral bracts 18 mm. long; dorsal sepal oblong-elliptic, rounded, lateral sepals connate to apex, behind lip; petals ovate-elliptic, rounded with short stem, densely papillose, with magenta speckles; lip oblong with 2 thickened keels down center, articulate to column foot; column short, 2–5 mm. long with terminal anther with 4 pollinia; ovary thick, stout, pedicellate, 1 cm. long.
First discovered in southern Florida in 1963. Flower reputed to resemble a snake's head with the mouth open. Found a few times growing on tree branches among other epiphytic plants in or at the margin of swamp forest. Flowers from February to May.

(*Continued on next text page*)

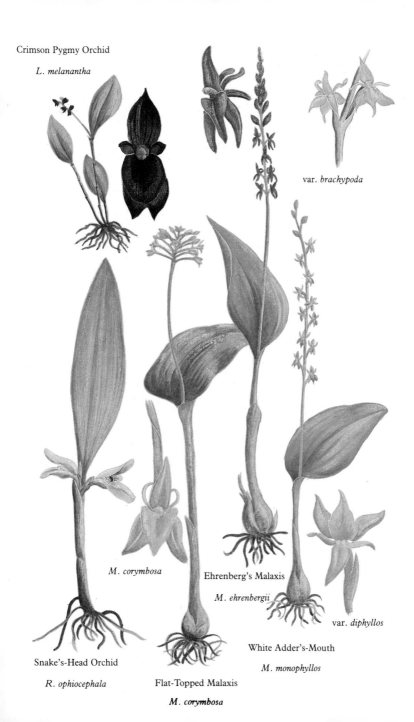

Crimson Pygmy Orchid

L. melanantha

var. *brachypoda*

M. corymbosa

Ehrenberg's Malaxis

M. ehrenbergii

var. *diphyllos*

White Adder's-Mouth

M. monophyllos

Snake's-Head Orchid

R. ophiocephala

Flat-Topped Malaxis

M. corymbosa

Bog Orchids *Malaxis*

A large genus of perhaps over 200 species with a worldwide distribution. Eight species occur in North America. The species in the group possess relatively soft green leaves rising from bulbous stem base; inflorescence in a terminal spike; flowers usually nonresupinate; sepals reflexed; petals small or filiform; lip variable, entire or three-lobed; column short and erect.

Flat-Topped Malaxis *Malaxis corymbosa* (S. Watson) Kuntze
10–25 cm., terrestrial, glabrous; stem swollen at base into pseudobulb; leaf solitary, cordate, about halfway up stem; inflorescence a corymbose spike of up to 40 crowded green flowers; floral bracts triangular, 2 mm. long; sepals ovate-elliptic, laterals oblique; petals very slender, recurved; lip directed downward, cordate, acuminate; column short, 1 mm. long; ovary slender, stalked, 3–12 mm. long; lower flowers with longest stalks.
Can be recognized by its corymbose raceme and flower pedicels up to 10 mm. long. A Mexican species that extends into the Huachuca Mountains of southern Arizona, where it grows in coniferous woodlands in damp humus. Flowers during August.

Ehrenberg's Malaxis *Malaxis ehrenbergii* (Reichenbach filius) Kuntze
20–45 cm., terrestrial, glabrous; stem base swollen into a pseudobulb; leaf solitary, ovate-elliptic, borne on lower half of stem, the petiolate base sheathing the stem; inflorescence a slender, lax spike of up to 60 reddish flowers; floral bracts lanceolate, 2 mm. long; sepals lanceolate-elliptic with revolute margins, lateral sepals oblique; petals linear, recurved; lip directed downward, ovate, acuminate; column minute; ovary short, pedicellate, 2.5 mm. long.
Identified by its slender spike of reddish to reddish purple flowers and in having flower pedicels only 3 mm. long. Another Mexican species that occurs in the mountains of southeastern Arizona and New Mexico. Grows on mountain slopes in coniferous woodland in humus. Flowers from July to September.

(Continued on next text page)

White Adder's-Mouth *Malaxis monophyllos* (Linnaeus) Swartz
Var. *brachypoda* (A. Gray) Morris & Eames

6–20 cm., terrestrial, glabrous; stem swollen at base to form pseudobulb; leaf solitary, ovate-elliptic on lower half of stem, its petiolate base sheathing the stem; inflorescence a slender, laxly flowered spike of up to 50 minute greenish white flowers; floral bracts lanceolate, 1.5 mm. long; dorsal sepal ovate-lanceolate with revolute margins, lateral sepals oblong-lanceolate, oblique; petals very slender, reflexed; lip directed downward, broadly triangular, three-lobed, with laterals auriculate, curved upward, median lobe acuminate; column short, 0.5 mm. long; ovary short, pedicellate.

Can be distinguished from *M. unifolia* in having middle lobe of lip longer than the laterals and downward-pointing lip. A northern species that ranges from southern Alaska and British Columbia across Canada to Newfoundland; occurs in the U.S. in the Great Lakes and northeastern regions. Locally abundant in the North in wet meadows, wooded swamps, and bog margins. Flowers from June to August.

Var. *diphyllos* (Chamisso) Luer from the Aleutian Islands has 2 or even 3 leaves, and the flower is nonresupinate, with the lip directed upward. Flowers from June to August; abundant.

Bog Orchid *Malaxis paludosa* (Linnaeus) Swartz
(Syn. *Hammarbya paludosa* [Linnaeus] Kuntze)
3–10 cm., terrestrial, glabrous; stem swollen at base in round pseudobulb with previous year's pseudobulb below; leaves two to four, ovate-elliptic, keeled, sometimes with tiny plantlets sprouting from tips of leaves; inflorescence a spike of laxly flowered or crowded yellow-green flowers, three to thirty-five in number; floral bracts minute, triangular; median sepal ovate-lanceolate, lateral sepals elliptic, oblique, reflexed; petals ovate-lanceolate, recurved; lip pointing upward, ovate; column minute, erect; ovary slender, pedicellate, 3 mm. long.
Distinguished by its two to four leaves, nonresupinate flowers, and small size. Apparently local and rare in North America, perhaps due in some part to the extreme difficulty of finding this tiny orchid in its sphagnum bog habitat. Ranges from Alaska to British Columbia, east to Ontario and Minnesota. Grows in sphagnum moss bogs, often half hidden by moss. Flowers from June to August.

Mountain Malaxis *Malaxis macrostachya* (Lexarza) Kuntze
(Syn. *Malaxis soulei* L. O. Williams)
10–40 cm., terrestrial, glabrous; stem swollen at base to form pseudobulb; leaf solitary, ovate to elliptic, its petiolate base sheathing the stem; inflorescence a spike of up to fifty greenish or whitish flowers on a stout rachis; floral bracts minute; sepals ovate to elliptic, lateral sepals oblique; petals slender, reflexed; lip uppermost, subquatrate with basal auricles, apex usually notched (sometimes obtuse) with small central tooth; column erect, 0.5 mm. long; ovary short, pedicellate, 2 mm. long.
Can be recognized by its "rat's tail" flower spike and notched or obtuse lip apex. A Central American and Mexican species that ranges into southern Arizona, New Mexico, and southwestern Texas. Grows on rocky slopes in open forest at considerable elevations. Flowers from July to October.

Little Orange-Lip *Malaxis spicata* Swartz
8–40 cm., terrestrial or semi-epiphytic; leaves two, ovate, glabrous, nearly opposite; stem swollen at base into pseudobulb; enveloped by leaf sheaths; inflorescence a slender, loosely flowered spike of up to fifty tiny green flowers; floral bracts triangular, 3 mm. long; median sepal ovate, convex, lateral sepals elliptic, curled; petals linear, recurved strongly; lip uppermost, orange-brown, cordate with basal lobes embracing the column; column minute with terminal anther; ovary slender, stalked, 5 mm. long.
Identified by its two leaves and orange lip directed upward. Locally not uncommon along the Atlantic seaboard from Virginia and North Carolina south to Florida. Grows in shade in the humus of thick woodlands and in forested swamps where it occurs semi-epiphytically on mossy stumps and logs. Flowers from January in Florida to August in the North.

Slender Malaxis *Malaxis tenuis* (S. Watson) Ames
5–20 cm., terrestrial, glabrous, stem swollen at base into pseudobulb; leaf solitary, ovate, its petiolate base sheathing the stem; inflorescence a cylindrical raceme, blunt at tip, with up to thirty-five narrow green flowers; floral bract triangular, 2 mm. long; median sepal lanceolate, lateral sepals lanceolate, oblique; petals very slender; lip uppermost, ovate-triangular, acuminate; column broad; ovary slender, pedicellate, 11 mm. long.
Distinguished by its acuminate lip and flower pedicels 10 mm. long. Mexican species that reaches the mountains of southern Arizona and New Mexico. Grows in humus on wooded hillsides. Flowers from July to October.

Green Adder's-Mouth *Malaxis unifolia* Michaux
8–20 cm., terrestrial; leaf solitary, ovate, its base sheathing the lower stem; base of stem developed into pseudobulb; inflorescence many-flowered, subumbellate, five to fifty tiny green flowers; floral bract triangular, 3 mm. long; sepals linear-lanceolate; petals linear, strongly recurved; lip pointed downward, cordate with apex bidentate with an intermediate tiny tooth; column minute with terminal anther; ovary slender, stalked, 3–10 mm. long.
Recognized by its solitary leaf, umbellate inflorescence, and resupinate lip. Distribution from eastern North America, north to Newfoundland, west to Great Lakes, south to Florida and Texas. Grows in damp situations in forest and woodlands and along wooded streams. Flowers from February in Florida to August in the North.

Bog Orchid

M. paludosa

Green Adder's-Mouth

M. unifolia

Mountain Malaxis

M. macrostachya

Little Orange-Lip

M. spicata

Slender Malaxis

M. tenuis

Fen Orchids *Liparis*

A large genus of some 250 mainly terrestrial orchids, distributed throughout the world in both temperate and tropical areas, with three species occurring in North America. Sheathed pseudobulb; rather fleshy green leaves; flowering stem with loosely flowered raceme; sepals and petals spreading; lip uppermost or pointing downward, varying from three-lobed to emarginate; column elongate, laterally winged; anther terminal.

Tall Liparis *Liparis elata* Lindley

20–50 cm., terrestrial to semi-epiphytic; pseudobulbs slightly compressed, conical; leaves three to seven, oblong-lanceolate, up to 25 cm. long, completely sheathing new pseudobulb and base of stem; inflorescence an erect stem from center of leaves with a laxly flowered terminal raceme of up to thirty small purplish flowers; floral bracts lanceolate, same length as ovary; dorsal sepal linear with revolute edges, lateral sepals linear-ovate; petals narrowly spatulate; lip deep purple, reddish or green with recurved edges; column curved and winged, bright green, tipped by bright green anther; ovary stout, purplish, stalked.

Can be recognized by its leaf rosette and tall flower spike. Known in North America only from western Florida. Grows in both dense swamp forest and hardwood forest. Flowers from July to September.

Fen Orchid *Liparis loeselii* (Linnaeus) L. C. Richard

6–25 cm., terrestrial, glabrous; pseudobulb ovoid enveloped in dead leaf sheaths; leaves two, basal, glossy green, sheathing base of stem and pseudobulb; inflorescence lax, three to twelve greenish yellow flowers; floral bracts minute; sepals and petals spreading; lip uppermost, entire, recurved; no spur; column 3 mm. long with terminal anther; ovary slender, 6 mm. long.

Can be identified by its two basal leaves, greenish yellow flowers, and lip less than 5 mm. long. Distribution in northeastern United States and adjacent areas of Canada, southern Manitoba, Ontario, Quebec, and Nova Scotia, through the Great Lakes states to New York and Pennsylvania, south to Virginia, with isolated localities in Missouri, Kansas, and Alabama. Grows in bogs, damp sand-dune slacks, lake margins, ravines, and damp sandy meadows. Flowers from May to August.

Mauve Sleekwort *Liparis lilifolia* (Linnaeus) L. C. Richard ex Lindley

10–25 cm., terrestrial, glabrous; pseudobulb ovoid, enveloped in dry sheaths; leaves two, basal, glossy green, sheathing stem and pseudobulb; inflorescence a lax raceme of up to twenty-seven pale purplish flowers; floral bracts minute; sepals pale green, spreading; petals very slender, purple, reflexed; lip obovate with pointed apex, translucent, pale purplish brown; column curved, slightly winged; anther terminal; ovary slender, more or less horizontal.

Distinguished by its two basal leaves and purplish brown lip over 8 mm. long. Range in northeastern United States from Minnesota and Wisconsin south to northern Arkansas, Mississippi, Alabama, and northern Georgia, east to the Atlantic coast. Grows in fairly open woodland, in ravines, and on the banks of woodland streams. Flowers from May to July.

Fen Orchid

L. loeselii

Tall Liparis

L. elata

Mauve Sleekwort

L. lilifolia

Crane-Fly Orchid *Tipularia*

A small genus of 3 species, 1 of which occurs in the eastern U.S. Characterized by a series of connected underground tubers that produce a leaf in autumn and a flowering stem in summer. Inflorescence an elongated lax raceme of greenish yellow to purplish flowers; sepals and petals free, but one petal tends to overlap the dorsal sepal; lip three-lobed with long slender spur; column with terminal anther.

Crane-Fly Orchid *Tipularia discolor* (Pursh) Nuttall
15–60 cm., terrestrial, glabrous; leaf solitary, dark green above, purple below, long-stalked, absent by flowering time; stem slender; inflorescence a lax raceme of 20–40 pale green and purplish flowers; sepals and petals greenish white with pale purplish markings, spreading; lip three-lobed, lateral lobes small and rounded, median lobe slender, spreading slightly at apex; spur slender, 22 mm. long; column 3–4 mm. long with terminal anther; ovary slender, more or less horizontal. Identified by absence of leaf at flowering time, long slender spur, and slightly asymmetrical flowers. Distribution from northeastern states west to Nebraska, south to Florida and eastern Texas. An elusive and uncommon orchid. Grows in both coniferous and deciduous forests, in hammocks in Florida, and along banks of streams. Flowers from June in the north of its range to September in the southern areas.

Calypso *Calypso*

A monotypic genus that is circumpolar in distribution. The plant has an oval or rounded bulbous corm, a single long-stemmed leaf, and a solitary pendent flower from the top of the stem. Sepals and petals spreading and ascending; lip a slipper-shaped inflated pouch; column with single anther bearing 2 pairs of flat, waxy pollinia fixed to a detachable viscidium.

Calypso *Calypso bulbosa* (Linnaeus) Oakes var. *americana* (R. Brown) Luer
10–20 cm., terrestrial, glabrous; leaf solitary, long-stalked, dark green; inflorescence a single pendent flower from tip of stem; floral bract lanceolate, pinkish, 10–12 mm. long; sepals and petals similar, linear-lanceolate, pink, spreading or ascending; lip inflated and slipper-shaped with prominent tuft of yellow hairs at base, lip sac marked with bright purple; column suborbicular, convex, pink; anther on the under surface with 2 pairs of pollinia; ovary slender, pedicellate.
Easily recognized by its pink sepals and petals and slipper-shaped lip. Distribution from southern half of Alaska east across Canada to Newfoundland; occurs locally in the West in Montana, Wyoming, Colorado, southeastern Utah, Arizona, and New Mexico at moderately high altitudes; in the northeast occurs rarely in the Great Lakes, east to New York and Nova Scotia. Grows in wet, mossy places in coniferous forest, marshes, and swamps. Flowers from May and June to early July.
Var. *occidentalis* (Holzinger) Calder & Taylor differs in having a small patch of white hairs instead of a yellow hair tuft on the lip, and its lip is mottled lavender-brown, not purple. Isolated in the West in the Cascade Mountains and adjacent areas west of the Rocky Mountains. Flowers from March to July.

Calypso

C. bulbosa

var. *occidentalis*

(Continued on next text page)

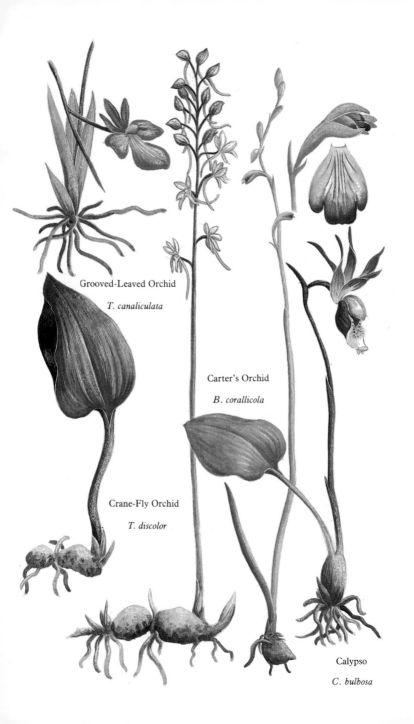

Grooved-Leaved Orchid

T. canaliculata

Carter's Orchid

B. corallicola

Crane-Fly Orchid

T. discolor

Calypso

C. bulbosa

Carter's Orchid *Basiphyllaea*

A small genus of 3 species found in the Bahamas and Greater Antilles. Collected in southeast Florida in 1906, but since that time does not seem to have been rediscovered. Plant is inconspicuous, a slender stem that rises from tuberous roots. Inflorescence an elongated raceme of small flowers; perianth segments free but not spreading; lip with 5 ridges; column with terminal anther with 4 pairs of pollinia.

Carter's Orchid *Basiphyllaea corallicola* (Small) Ames
10–40 cm., terrestrial, glabrous; leaf solitary, sometimes 2 leaves, linear; stem erect, slender; inflorescence an extended spike of 3–10 flowers that do not open completely, green with crimson on lip; sepals and petals converge over lip, yellowish green; lip three-lobed, yellowish with crimson wash, 5 ridges in center; column slender with bright crimson terminal anther; ovary slender.
In the U.S. recorded only from southeastern Florida. Grows in limestone rocks. Flowers in October and November.

Grooved-Leaved Orchid *Tetramicra*

Mainly West Indian in distribution, a small genus of a dozen species, one of which was recorded in 1961 from southeastern Florida. Epiphytic on bases of shrubs; roots an elongated creeping rhizome; leaves 2–5, linear, fleshy, and deeply grooved; flowering stem long and slender with 2–8 flowers in a simple raceme; floral bract ovate, 3 mm. long; sepals and petals deep green, lateral sepals hidden behind lip; lip deeply three-lobed; column winged with terminal anther containing 8 waxy pollinia.

Grooved-Leaved Orchid *Tetramicra canaliculata* (Aublet) Urban
Epiphytic; leaves 3–5, linear, fleshy, grooved; inflorescence a slender flowering stalk up to 70–80 cm. long with a few bracts, bearing up to 8 flowers in a simple raceme; floral bract ovate, 3 mm. long; sepals and petals dark green, spreading, lateral sepals hidden below lip; lip bright rose-pink, deeply three-lobed, central lobe with 5 streaks, middle streak yellow, side streaks deep mauve; column winged with terminal anther; ovary slender, 20 mm. long.
Easily recognized by its conspicuous, flat, three-lobed lip. Known only from the southeast coast of Florida, where it has been found growing on the basal branches of rosemary bushes. Flowers in May and June.

Epidendrums *Epidendrum*

A very large genus of mainly tropical South American species of which seven species are found in North America. Mainly an epiphytic group. Typically plants have slender leafy stems; flowers relatively small and not very showy; inflorescence either a simple raceme or in a panicle from end of flowering stem; sepals and petals free, lip expanded; column rounded, terminate operculate anther.

Brown Epidendrum *Epidendrum anceps* Jacquin
Epiphytic, erect, with leafy stems up to 110 cm. tall; leaves five to twelve, normally green but sometimes suffused with red; inflorescence a terminal umbelliform raceme, densely flowered, up to twenty-five firm-textured brown, orange-brown, or olive flowers; floral bract lanceolate, 5 mm. long; sepals and petals spreading; lip indistinctly three-lobed, heart-shaped, apex emarginate, median lobe with ridge; column 5 mm. long, dilated toward apex; anther terminal; ovary slender, pedicellate, 15 mm. long.

(Continued on next text page)

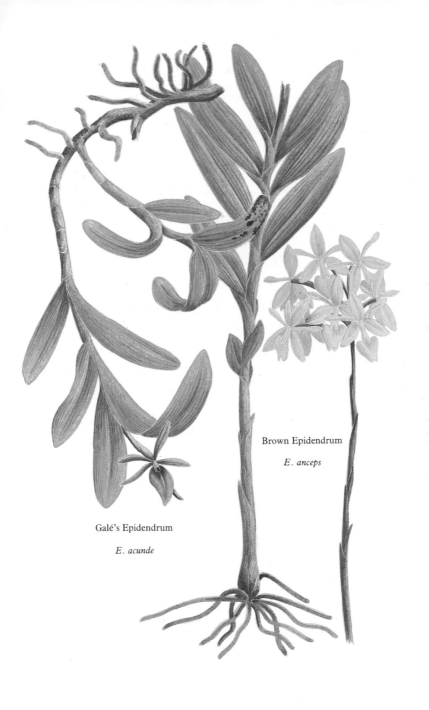

Brown Epidendrum

E. anceps

Galé's Epidendrum

E. acunde

Distinguished by its umbelliform raceme and lip less than 9 mm. wide. A fairly common epiphytic orchid in southern Florida. Grows on horizontal branches and vertical tree trunks in forests, swamps, and hammocks. Flowers mainly from January to July, but blooms may be found at any time of year.

Galé's Epidendrum *Epidendrum acunde* Dressler
Epiphytic, pendent, with stems over 1 m. tall; roots numerous and slender; stem pendent, branching; leaves rigid, alternating at tip, two to six on each branch; inflorescence one to three brownish flowers from apex of branch; sepals greenish brown, revolute; petals similar, also revolute; lip entire, greenish brown suffused with purple; column 4.5 mm. long with terminal anther; ovary sessile, slender, concealed by floral bracts.

Distinguished by having flowers in a compact raceme at end of pendent stem; floral parts about 10 mm. long. Species first discovered in the Fahkahatchee Swamp in southern Florida in 1962. Occurs in dense swamp forest, growing high on the larger trees. Flowers during May and June.

Greenfly Orchid *Epidendrum conopseum* R. Brown in Aiton
Epiphytic, erect; leafy stems up to 30 cm. long; roots numerous, slender; leaves two to four, dark green; inflorescence a lax raceme of up to eighteen yellowish green flowers; sepals oblanceolate; petals slender, spatulate; lip three-lobed, laterals and middle lobe subquadrate, 6 mm. long, two blunt protuberances at base; column 7 mm. long, dilated toward apex; anther terminal; ovary slender, 20 mm. long.

Distinguished by its prominent lateral lip lobes and racemose flowering stem. *E. conopseum* has the widest distribution of the genus and occurs locally as far north as North Carolina and west to Louisiana. Normally found high in deciduous trees. Flowers mainly from September to February, but may bloom sporadically in other months.

Umbelled Epidendrum *Epidendrum difforme* Jacquin
Epiphytic, pendent; leafy stems up to 30 cm. long; roots numerous; leaves five to ten, glossy green, thick; inflorescence a short peduncle at end of stem, racemose umbelliform, pendent; flowers greenish, variable in size and shape; sepals and petals slender, spreading; lip indistinctly three-lobed, lateral lobes rounded, median lobe emarginate; column 8 mm. long, dilated toward apex; anther terminal; ovary slender, pedicellate.

Distinguished by its pendent umbelliform raceme and lip more than 9 mm. wide. A common species in the hammocks and forests of southern Florida. Flowers mainly from August to November, but blooms may be found at any time.

Greenfly Orchid

E. conopseum

Umbelled Epidendrum

E. difforme

Night-Scented Epidendrum *Epidendrum nocturnum* Jacquin

Epiphytic, erect; leafy stems up to 1 m. long; leaves four to ten, dark green; inflorescence up to five flowers, blooming one or two at a time on terminal peduncle; sepals and petals long and slender, spreading, pale yellow; lip deeply three-lobed, lateral lobes obliquely ovate, median lobe filiform, white with pair of yellow lamellae toward base; column 18 mm. long, dilated toward apex with terminal anther; ovary slender, 8 mm. long.

Easily recognized by its deeply three-lobed white lip. Not uncommon in the forests of southern Florida. Grows on tree branches and also on trunks of royal palms. Flowers mainly from July to December, but blooms may be found at other times. Strongly fragrant at night.

Rigid Epidendrum *Epidendrum rigidum* Jacquin

Epiphytic, ascending; leafy stems up to 20 cm. long; leaves two to six, green, alternate; inflorescence three to ten nonresupinate green flowers from triangular floral bracts; sepals obovate; petals linear; lip uppermost, broadly ovate; column denticulate at apex; anther green with two pollinia; ovary sessile, stout, 1 cm. long.

Can be identified by its small green flowers, entire lip, and flowers borne at intervals from an erect stem. Common in forests and hammocks in southern Florida. Grows on tree branches, often near the ground. Flowers from October to May.

Pine-Cone Epidendrum *Epidendrum strobiliferum* Reichenbach filius

Epiphytic, pendent; leafy stems up to 18 cm. long; leaves two to eight, green, sometimes tinged with reddish brown, alternate; inflorescence terminal, three or four pale yellow nonresupinate flowers with ovaries concealed by large floral bracts; sepals ovate; petals linear oblanceolate; lip uppermost, ovate, concave with pair of white lamellae toward base; column small, dentate above anther; ovary sessile, thick.

Can be recognized by its small yellow flowers borne in a compact pendent raceme. A very uncommon species known from the Fahkahatchee Swamp in southern Florida. Grows on tree trunks, often near the ground. Flowers during October and November and probably at other times.

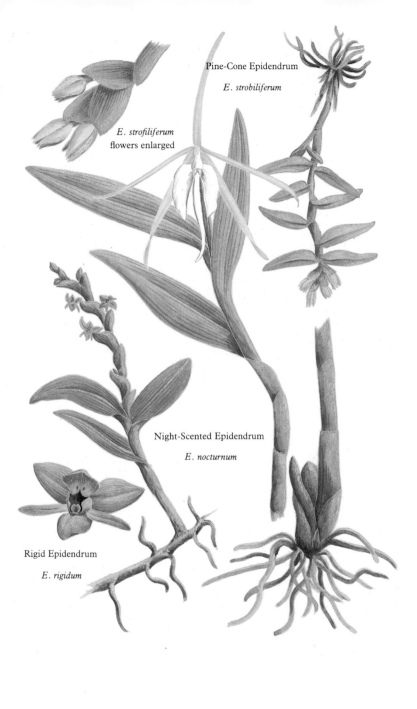

Pine-Cone Epidendrum

E. strobiliferum

E. strofiliferum
flowers enlarged

Night-Scented Epidendrum

E. nocturnum

Rigid Epidendrum

E. rigidum

Encyclia Orchids *Encyclia*

A large genus, previously lumped with *Epidendrum*. Most species possess pseudobulbs from which the leaves and stem arise. Inflorescence varies from a simple raceme to a multibranched panicle; sepals and petals free; lip either free or partially united with column; lip enfolds column, forming a tubular nectary. Center of abundance in Mexico and the West Indies, with four species occurring in Florida.

Dollar Orchid *Encyclia boothiana* (Lindley) Dressler
Var. *erythronioides* (Small) Luer

Epiphytic; pseudobulbs somewhat compressed, rounded; leaves one to three, bright green, glossy, spreading from apex of pseudobulb; inflorescence a slender flowering stalk up to 30 cm. long; lax raceme of one to twelve waxy, widely spreading flowers; sepals and petals greenish yellow with reddish purple markings; lip whitish to pale yellowish green, barely three-lobed, lateral margins downcurved; column dentate at apex with three yellow anthers; ovary slender, pedicellate.

Can be recognized by flower pattern and compressed, rounded pseudobulb. Owing to destruction of habitat the Dollar Orchid is nowadays an uncommon species, found on some of the Florida Keys and Cape Sable. Its habitat is swamp forest where it grows on various hardwood trees, usually quite near the ground. Flowers during August and September.

Clamshell Orchid *Encyclia cochleata* (Linnaeus) Dressler
Var. *triandra* (Ames) Dressler

Epiphytic; pseudobulbs elongated, somewhat compressed; leaves one to three, from apex of pseudobulb; inflorescence slender stem up to 40 cm. long with a lax raceme of up to ten nonresupinate flowers; sepals and petals slender, yellowish, often with a few purple spots at base; lip uppermost, broadly heart-shaped, concave, apiculate, incurved at base, deep purple or purplish brown with pale veins; column erect, thick, yellowish with purple speckles, dentate at apex with central large orange anther plus a smaller anther on each side; ovary slender, pedicellate.

Easily recognized by its uppermost, shell-like lip and elongated pseudobulbs. Not uncommon in the wet forests of southern Florida. Flowers from September to April.

Clamshell Orchid

E. cochleata

Dollar Orchid

E. boothiana

Dwarf Encyclia *Encyclia pygmaea* (Hooker) Dressler
Epiphytic; pseudobulb round, slender, 2–8 cm. long, 3–8 mm. wide, erect; leaves two or three, green, elliptic, obliquely spreading from apex of pseudobulb; inflorescence one to three yellowish green flowers, sessile on short peduncle between bases of leaves; floral bracts acuminate; middle sepal pale yellowish green, oblanceolate, lateral sepals similar, acuminate; petals pale yellowish green, linear; lip uppermost, white, three-lobed, lateral lobes curving upward, median lobe pointed, tip purple; column 2 mm. long, three prongs at apex surrounding orange anther; ovary narrow, pedicellate.
Can be recognized by slender, round pseudobulb, small size, and apiculate central lobe of lip. Known only from the Fahkahatchee Swamp in southern Florida. Grows on branches of trees deep in the swamp. Flowers from October to February.

Florida Butterfly Orchid *Encyclia tampensis* (Lindley) Small
Epiphytic, glabrous; pseudobulbs leafy, ovoid; leaves one to three, dark green, linear-lanceolate, keeled, from apex of pseudobulb; inflorescence a flowering stem rising from apex of pseudobulb, slender, up to 80 cm. long; laxly few- to many-flowered, up to forty-five flowers, in a raceme or panicle, flowers showy; floral bracts minute; sepals and petals similar, oblanceolate, spreading, variable in color, green, yellow, pale brown, sometimes with purplish tinge; lip deeply three-lobed, lateral lobes curved upward, veined mauve or magenta, median lobe suborbicular, white with central purple or magenta patch, sometimes with an all-purple lip; column winged with terminal anther, 10 mm. long; ovary slender, pedicellate.
One of the most beautiful of the North American epiphytic orchids, relatively common in many localities in Florida where it occurs in swamp forests, in hammocks, and on isolated trees in exposed situations. Flowering peak is in June and July, but blooms may be found sporadically throughout the year.

Polystachyas *Polystachya*

Mainly a tropical family having its center of abundance in Africa and Asia with a few species occurring in the American tropics and one in southern Florida. Pseudobulbs epiphytic, slender; inflorescence apical raceme simple or paniculate with rather small nonresupinate flowers; uppermost lip variously shaped; column with more or less prominent foot to which lateral sepals and lip are attached; anther terminal.

Pale-Flowered Polystachya *Polystachya flavescens* (Lindley) J. J. Smith
(Syn. *Polystachya luteola* [Swartz] Hooker)
Epiphytic, leafy; pseudobulb slender, conical, about 5 cm. long; leaves two to five, green, rather thin, linear-lanceolate; inflorescence a flowering stem from pseudobulb apex, up to 40 cm. long, compressed, usually branched from upper side, flowers nonresupinate, greenish yellow, in fairly lax raceme, ten or so to each branch of flowering stem; floral bracts small, 3 mm. long; middle sepal ovate, concave, lateral sepals with margins adnate to column foot, forming a prominent mentum; petals narrow, linear-spatulate; lip uppermost in flower, hinged downward from column foot, three-lobed, lateral lobes incurved, middle lobe slightly dilated at apex; white pubescent crest toward base; column 2 mm. long but with a foot twice as long; anther terminal; ovary slender, pedicellate, 5 mm. long.
In the United States found only in southern Florida, growing high on branches of forest trees. Flowers most frequently in September and October, but blooms may be found at almost any time of year.

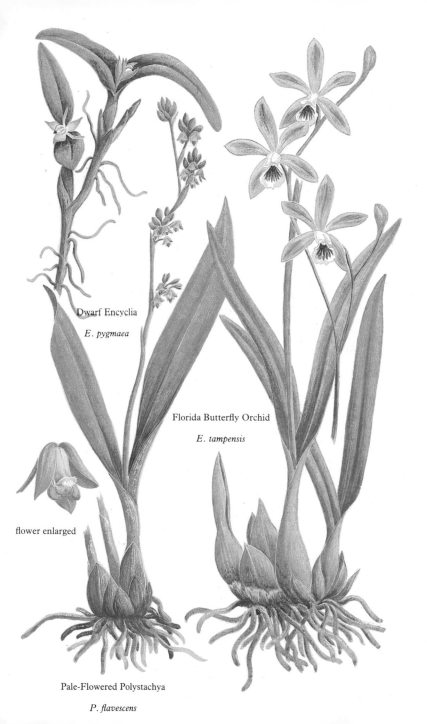

Dwarf Encyclia

E. pygmaea

Florida Butterfly Orchid

E. tampensis

flower enlarged

Pale-Flowered Polystachya

P. flavescens

Helmet Orchid *Galeandra*

A group of about twenty-five Central and South American species of which one occurs in Florida. Genus contains both epiphytic and terrestrial species. Most have a stout flowering stem covered by membranous sheaths; flowers relatively large, paniculate or in a simple raceme; sepals and petals free and spreading; lip forming a large broad spur at base; column with short foot, small apical wings, and terminal anther.

Helmet Orchid *Galeandra beyrichii* Reichenbach filius

30 cm.–1 m., terrestrial, glabrous; stem robust, pseudobulbous at base with sheathing scales; leaves one or two, erect, lanceolate, three-ribbed, absent at time of flowering; inflorescence a terminal lax raceme of a few to twelve greenish flowers; floral bracts lanceolate, 10 mm. long; sepals and petals oblanceolate, yellowish green; lip white with green stripes, base produced into a short broad spur, apex rounded, pubescent, with wavy margin marked with magenta just inside margin; column with indistinct foot; anther terminal, green with one pair of pollinia; ovary slender, pedicellate, 2 cm. long.

First discovered in the United States in 1946 in Costello Hammock, southern Florida. Further plants discovered in subsequent years, but *G. beyrichii* remains a very rare species. Flowers during September and October.

Puttyroot *Aplectrum*

Terrestrial scapose orchid growing from globose tubers, these preconnected by a slender rhizome; leaf solitary, appearing in winter and persisting to spring; inflorescence a fairly lax terminal raceme; sepals and petals free, more or less spreading; lip three-lobed, free, with ridges toward base; column very slightly curved, compressed; terminal anther bearing four pollinia. The tubers of this orchid have been used for medicinal purposes in the past.

Puttyroot *Aplectrum hyemale* (Muhlenberg & Willdenow) Nuttall

25–50 cm., terrestrial, glabrous; leaves and later flowering stalks rising from series of moniliform, glutinous corms, connected by slender stolons; leaf solitary, stalked, elliptic, appearing in autumn and persisting until spring; inflorescence a lax raceme of up to fifteen flowers; flowers variable, whitish, greenish or yellowish, marked with pale magenta; sepals and petals similar, oblanceolate, tinged magenta; lip three-lobed, obovate, lateral lobes ovate, middle lobe expanded with slightly wavy margin, white with violet markings, three ridges toward base; column compressed, pale green with purple spots; anther terminal; ovary pedicellate, 8–11 mm. long.

Occurs in the northeastern states, west to the Great Lakes region, south to Arkansas, Mississippi, Alabama, and Georgia. Grows in wet soil in wooded areas, peat bogs, moist ravines, and moist woodlands. Flowers in May and June.

Gowen's Orchid *Govenia*

A small group of South American terrestrial orchids, one of which ranges into southern Florida. Characterized by a tuberlike pseudobulb with semi-inflated leaf sheaths at base of leaves and stem; leaves two, plicate; inflorescence a simple raceme with a few to many flowers; dorsal sepal concave and longer than lateral sepals, which are falcate and join the column foot to form a small mentum; petals also falcate, lodged below dorsal sepal; lip short, slightly curved, simple; column curved with a short foot; anther terminal.

Gowen's Orchid *Govenia utriculata* (Swartz) Lindley

20–50 cm., terrestrial; leaves two, elliptic, plicate, articulated with two erect tubular leaf sheaths, 10–20 cm. long; inflorescence a flowering stem from tuber, between basal sheaths, lax raceme of five to fifteen white flowers that do not open completely; floral bracts lanceolate, 25 mm. long; sepals obovate, lateral sepals falcate; petals obovate, lightly marked with purple specks on inside; lip slightly curved, simple with marginal purplish brown spots; column curved with short column foot, obscurely winged, suffused and mottled with pink; anther terminal; ovary white, slender, pedicellate.

Discovered in Everglades National Park in 1957 in a dense hammock in shade. A very rare species in North America. Flowers during November and December in Florida.

Gowen's Orchid

G. utriculata

Helmet Orchid

G. beyrichii

Puttyroot

A. hyemale

Cock's-Comb Orchids *Hexalectris*

A genus of seven species of saprophytic orchids of which five occur in the southern United States. Characterized by distinctive branched and annulated rhizomes from which arise a leafless stem. Inflorescence a lax raceme of colorful flowers; sepals and petals free, spreading; lip three-lobed with fleshy longitudinal ridges down the center of the middle lobe; column narrowly winged toward apex; anther terminal.

Greenman's Cock's-Comb *Hexalectris grandiflora* (A. Richards & Galeotti) L. O. Williams
30–60 cm., terrestrial, saprophytic, glabrous; stem leafless, reddish, erect with a few widely spaced bracts; inflorescence a lax raceme of up to fifteen well-spread bright pink flowers; floral bract ovate, 10 mm. long; dorsal and lateral sepals oblong; petals oblanceolate, oblique; lip deeply three-lobed, lateral lobes incurved, median lobe fan-shaped with deep pink margins, five longitudinal fleshy ridges toward base; column pink, curved, narrowly winged; anther terminal; ovary short, pedicellate, 15 mm. long.
Can be recognized by its deeply three-lobed lip with lamellae smooth and straight and by its bright pink flowers with sepals and petals not revolute. Known in the United States only from western Texas, where it has been found growing in the beds of canyons in semi-shade. Flowers from May to August.

Shining Cock's Comb *Hexalectris nitida* L. O. Williams
15–30 cm., terrestrial, saprophytic, glabrous; stem leafless, stout with few bracts, reddish mauve; inflorescence a loosely or densely flowered raceme of up to twenty five small flowers; floral bracts lanceolate, 6 mm. long; sepals and petals spreading, recurved, shiny pinkish brown with brownish veining; lip shallowly three-lobed, longer than it is wide, lateral lobes white, rounded, incurved, central lobe bright purple, wavy at margin, five longitudinal purple ridges toward base; column white, curved, narrowly winged with terminal anther; ovary stout, pedicellate, 15 mm. long.
Distinguished by its shallowly lobed lip, which is less than 10 mm. long, and by its recurved sepals and petals. Known in the United States only from southwestern Texas, where it has been found in the Chisos and Glass mountains. Grows on forested mountain slopes and in dry creek beds. Flowers from June to August.

Correll's Cock's-Comb *Hexalectris revoluta* Correll
25–30 cm., terrestrial, saprophytic, glabrous; leafless; stem erect, dull purplish, with a few widely spaced bracts; inflorescence a widely spaced spike with up to twelve brown and mauve flowers; floral bract slender, 10 mm. long; sepals and petals pale purplish brown with parallel veins, apices revolute; lip deeply three-lobed, broadly elliptic, lateral lobes white, veined with crimson, incurved, central lobe magenta, truncate, three low white ridges toward base of lip; column white to mauve below, curved, narrowly winged with terminal yellow anther; ovary slender, pedicellate, 18 mm. long.
Can be recognized by deeply three-lobed lip; smooth, straight lip ridges; brownish flowers; and revolute sepals and petals. A very rare orchid; in the United States known only in southwestern Texas. Grows in shade in oak groves that line rocky stream beds of higher altitudes in the mountains. Flowers from June to August.

Crested Coral-Root *Hexalectris spicata* (Walter) Barnhart
25–80 cm., terrestrial, saprophytic, glabrous; stem erect, brown or purplish, with a few bracts; inflorescence a loosely flowered spike of up to twenty five showy blooms; floral bract ovate, 8 mm. long; sepals and petals pale buff-brown with purple veining, oblanceolate, spreading; lip shallowly three-lobed, whitish with purple veins, ovate, lateral lobes angled, incurved, central lobe subtruncate with wavy margin, five to seven fleshy purplish ridges toward base; column curved, white with terminal anther; ovary short, pedicellate, 9 mm. long.
The least rare of this genus, *H. spicata* ranges from Virginia, Kentucky and Missouri, south to Florida, Texas, New Mexico, and Arizona. Grows in fairly open deciduous forest. Flowers from April in the South to August in Virginia.

(Continued on next text page)

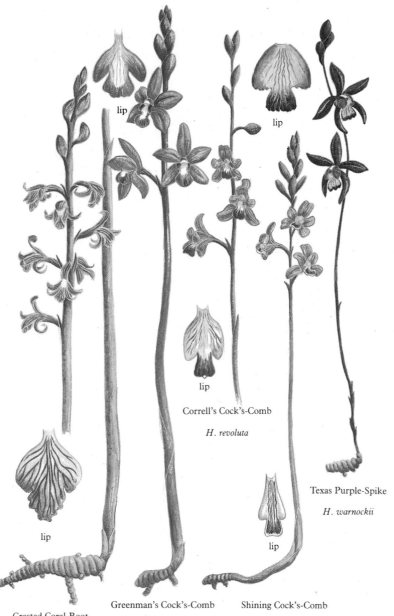

lip

lip

lip

Correll's Cock's-Comb

H. revoluta

lip

Texas Purple-Spike

H. warnockii

lip

lip

Crested Coral-Root

H. spicata

Greenman's Cock's-Comb

H. grandiflora

Shining Cock's-Comb

H. nitida

Texas Purple-Spike *Hexalectris warnockii* Ames & Correll
10–30 cm., terrestrial, saprophytic; leafless; stem slender, erect, reddish brown with few bracts; inflorescence a lax spike of up to ten crimson-brown flowers; sepals and petals deep maroon, spreading; lip deeply three-lobed, lateral lobes ovate, incurved, pale pink or whitish with magenta veining, central lobe maroon with crenulate margins, five yellow wavy ridges toward base to apex; column white, purplish below, curved, narrowly winged with terminal anther; ovary slender, pedicellate.
Can be recognized by its slender habit, deeply three-lobed lip, and denticulate, wavy lip lamellae. Found only in mountain areas of southern and central Texas and southeastern Arizona, growing in semi-shade below oaks and cedars along rocky creek beds. Flowers from June to August; rare.

Coral-Roots *Corallorhiza*

A group of ten saprophytic orchids of which six species occur in North America. Root system of fragile, branched, coral-like rhizomes; flowering stem with few membranous sheaths; raceme laxly flowered, floral bracts small; flowers more or less pendent; lateral sepals more or less spreading, dorsal sepal and petals somewhat incurved; lip entire, toothed at base, or three-lobed; pair of variable prominences toward base of lip; column compressed with terminal anther.

Spotted Coral-Root *Corallorhiza maculata* (Rafinesque) Rafinesque
15–80 cm., terrestrial, saprophytic, leafless, glabrous; stem erect, with few membranous sheaths, variously colored, yellowish, brownish, reddish, or tinged purple; inflorescence a loosely flowered raceme of up to forty flowers; floral bracts lanceolate, 3 mm. long; sepals similar in color to stem, oblanceolate, lateral sepals oblique, spreading slightly, at base conjoined to form small mentum below base of lip; petals paler than sepals; lip ovate, three-lobed, white, usually with few magenta spots, lateral lobes small, directed forward, central lobe expanded with toothed and undulate margin, pair of low longitudinal lamellae toward base; column 3–5 mm. long, curved, yellowish, with terminal anther; ovary short, pedicellate.
Can be recognized by three-lobed lip, large size (over 15 cm. tall), lip 5–9 mm. long, and lateral sepals not spreading widely. Widely distributed from British Columbia across Canada to Newfoundland; western, northern, and northeastern United States, south to California, Arizona, New Mexico, and Texas. Grows in shady coniferous and deciduous woodland; fairly common. Flowers from April to September.

Western Coral-Root *Corallorhiza mertensiana* Bongard
15–60 cm., terrestrial, saprophytic, glabrous; leafless; stem erect with some membranous sheaths, reddish or reddish mauve; inflorescence a laxly flowered terminal raceme of up to forty flowers; floral bracts minute; sepals oblanceolate, purplish brown, lateral sepals oblique and reflexed, bases joined and forming a 1 mm. mentum below base of lip; petals oblanceolate, pale purplish brown, sometimes with purple spots, petals and dorsal sepal connivent; lip bright claret red, elliptic-obovate, with toothed margin, entire or with very small lateral lobes at base, lip recurved near base, two low, parallel lamellae toward base of lip; column purplish yellow, slender with terminal anther; ovary short pedicellate.
Distinguished by its bright claret red lip, spreading lateral sepals, and column 6–8 mm. long. Western distribution, from extreme southern Alaska and British Columbia south to northern California, east to Wyoming and Colorado. Grows in humus in damp coniferous forests and subalpine woodlands; sometimes in drier forest and along boggy streams; mainly in mountains in south of range. Flowers from June to August.

Autumn Coral-Root *Corallorhiza odontorhiza* (Willdenow) Nuttall
10–20 cm., terrestrial, saprophytic; leafless; stem yellowish or tinged purple, erect, slender with swollen bulblike base; some tubular sheaths; inflorescence a laxly flowered raceme of five to fifteen small flowers; floral bracts minute; sepals and petals purplish green, lanceolate, converging above lip; lip entire, broadly ovate, white with purple spots, margin undulate, recurved; column 2 mm. long with terminal anther; ovary stout, pedicellate.

(Continued on next text page)

flower

flower

lip

lip

lip

lip

Western Coral-Root

C. mertensiana

Northern Coral-Root

C. trifida

Spotted Coral-Root

C. maculata

Autumn Coral-Root

C. odontorhiza

Distinguished by its entire lip without involute margins, stem with bulblike base, and sepals and petals less than 5 mm. long. Distributed commonly through eastern United States south to northern Florida and eastern Texas. Grows in humus of both deciduous and coniferous forests. Flowers from August to October.

Northern Coral-Root *Corallorhiza trifida* Chatelain

8–30 cm., terrestrial, saprophytic, glabrous; leafless; stem erect, yellowish to greenish white with a few tubular sheaths; inflorescence a loosely flowered raceme of up to twenty small flowers; floral bracts minute; dorsal sepal oblanceolate, yellowish green, lateral sepals linear-oblanceolate, curved, yellowish green; petals pale greenish, sometimes tinged purplish, oblanceolate; lip white, usually with a few purple spots or suffusion, three-lobed, lateral lobes short and triangular, median lobe expanded, rounded to truncate with undulate margin; column curved, 4 mm. long with terminal anther; ovary short, pedicellate, 8 mm. long.

Distinguished by its small size and three-lobed lip, which is only 3–5 mm. long. A common species with a circumpolar distribution. North American distribution ranges from Alaska and the Aleutian Islands across Canada to Newfoundland and southern Greenland; in western United States from Washington and Oregon southeast to northern New Mexico; also east from Washington through Great Lakes states to northeastern states. Grows among low vegetation on tundra, in woods and meadows and farther south in sphagnum bogs and wet woods. Flowers from May to August.

Striped Coral-Root *Corallorhiza striata* Lindley

15–50 cm., terrestrial, saprophytic, glabrous; leafless; stem erect, stout, largely concealed by membranous sheaths, purplish; inflorescence a laxly flowered raceme of up to thirty-five flowers; floral bracts ovate, 3 mm. long; sepals yellowish pink with crimson veining, linear oblong; petals similar, elliptic-oblanceolate; lip entire, elliptic-obovate, recurved near base, involute, 8–12 mm. long, deep crimson-purple or whitish with purple stripes; column curved, 5 mm. long with terminal anther; ovary short, pedicellate, 10–15 mm. long.

Widely distributed from southern half of British Columbia across Canada to New Brunswick; western United States from Washington to California; also Montana, Wyoming, Colorado, southern Arizona, New Mexico, South Dakota, southern Oklahoma, and the Great Lakes states. Not an uncommon species in open forests and woodland, favoring limestone areas; also found in canyons and along wooded streams. Flowers from May to August.

Var. *vreelandii* (Rydberg) L. O. Williams is similar to typical plants but smaller, growing to 25 cm., and with smaller flowers, which are yellowish brown marked with dull purple. Known only from northern California and Colorado. Flowers from May to August.

Spring Coral-Root *Corallorhiza wisteriana* Conrad

10–30 cm., terrestrial, saprophytic, glabrous; leafless; stem erect, slender, yellowish to pale purple, with membranous sheaths on lower part; inflorescence a loosely flowered spike of five to twenty-five small flowers that open incompletely; floral bracts minute; sepals and petals converge over lip, greenish to yellowish with mauve or brownish suffusion; lip entire, white spotted with pink or magenta, without involute margins; column 5 mm. long with terminal anther; ovary stout, pedicellate, 6 mm. long.

An uncommon southern species, in the West found in southwestern Wyoming, Colorado, Utah, Arizona, and New Mexico; in the southeast from Pennsylvania and Virginia south to Florida and Texas. Grows in shady hardwood and coniferous forests, in swampy woodland, on edges of cypress swamps, in subalpine meadows, and along banks of streams and rivers. Flowers from December in its southern stations to August in the north of its range.

(Continued on next text page)

lip

Spring Coral-Root

C. wisteriana

flower

Striped Coral-Root

C. striata

Rat-Tailed Orchid

B. pachyrhachis

Rat-Tailed Orchid *Bulbophyllum*

A large genus of some five hundred species, most of which occur in Africa and Asia. A few are found in the American tropics, and one has reached Florida. Characterized by short pseudobulbs bearing one or two leaves; pseudobulbs produced along creeping rhizome; flowers usually small; lip fleshy and hinged to column foot; column short with terminal anther.

Rat-Tailed Orchid *Bulbophyllum pachyrhachis* (A. Richard) Grisebach
Epiphytic, glabrous; pseudobulb ovoid, green, three-to-five angled; leaves two, from apex of pseudobulb, linear-oblong, keeled; inflorescence a stalk pendent from base of pseudobulb, green with purple flecks, spike of up to thirty spaced sessile flowers, greenish with purplish markings; floral bract triangular, 3–5 mm. long; bracteoles three, oblanceolate, 3 mm. long; dorsal sepal ovate, acuminate, lateral sepals ovate, oblique, acuminate, adnate to column foot; petals oblong with maroon spotting; lip entire, red, fleshy, curved downward, articulated to column foot by claw; column 2–5 mm. long with a foot 2 mm. long, three-toothed at apex; anther terminal; ovary sessile, 1 mm. long.
Discovered in the Fahkahatchee Swamp in southern Florida in 1956. A very rare species. Flowers during November and December in Florida.

Pine-Pinks *Bletia*

A Central and South American genus of which two species occur in southern Florida. Elongated, pleated leaves and flowering stem produced independently from fleshy corm; sepals and petals free; lip entire or three-lobed, median lobe may be bilobed, its center with lamellae or papillae; column curved and winged; anther terminal.

Pine-Pink *Bletia purpurea* (Lamarck) A. de Candolle
100–150 cm., terrestrial to semi-epiphytic, glabrous; pseudobulb ovoid, solid; leaves three to five, green, linear-lanceolate, plicate, from apex of pseudobulb; inflorescence an erect slender stem, purplish, loosely flowered raceme or sometimes branched with three to eighty showy pink flowers; floral bract lanceolate, 5 mm. long; dorsal sepal oblong, pink, lateral sepals elliptic, pink, sometimes with a yellow stripe; petals ovate, pink, incurved over column; lip deeply three-lobed, pink with magenta veining, lateral lobes incurved, median lobe truncate with bright yellow lamellae, margin crenate, deep magenta, 18 mm. long; column white, curved, slightly winged, with column foot; anther terminal; ovary slender, pedicellate.
Sepals and petals about 2 cm. long; smaller than *B. patula*. In United States found only in southern Florida. Habitat varies from dry coniferous woodland where plants grow in humus-filled fissures in rock, or they may grow epiphytically on stumps and logs in swamp forest. Flowers from December to May.

Haiti Pine-Pink *Bletia patula* Hooker
40–160 cm., terrestrial, glabrous; leaves three to five, green, linear-lanceolate, pleated, from apex of pseudobulb; inflorescence a flowering stem produced from corm, a laxly flowered raceme of ten to twenty rose-purple flowers; floral bract 5 mm. long; dorsal sepal oblanceolate, rose-pink, lateral sepals similar but oblique; petals pale pink, spatulate; lip obovate, shallowly three-lobed, lateral lobes rounded, pink-veined magenta, median lobe rounded with wavy margin, deep purple with several white lamellae; column white, 23 mm. long; anther terminal; ovary pedicellate, 30 mm. long.
Sepals and petals about 3 cm. long; larger than *B. purpurea*. First discovered in United States in 1947 in coniferous woodland near Miami, the plants growing terrestrially. This locality has now been built over, and it is not certain that this species still exists in Florida. Flowers from March to May.

(Continued on next text page)

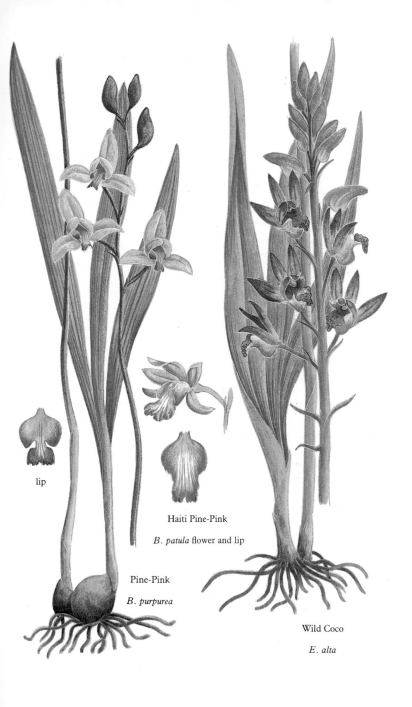

lip

Haiti Pine-Pink

B. patula flower and lip

Pine-Pink

B. purpurea

Wild Coco

E. alta

Wild Cocos *Eulophia*

A large genus, some two hundred species of mainly terrestrial orchids. Center of abundance in Africa, but two species occur in southeastern United States. Flowering stems and leaves produced independently from fleshy corms; stem with a fairly laxly flowered raceme, sepals and petals usually free, but in some species lateral sepals are joined to base of column from which the lip is hinged; lip three-lobed, concave, lateral lobes upcurved around column, median lobe with lamellae; column short, often winged; anther terminal.

Wild Coco *Eulophia alta* (Linnaeus) Fawcett & Rendle
50–150 cm., terrestrial, glabrous; leaves four to six, green, linear-lanceolate, pleated, up to 100 cm. long, rising from fleshy corms; inflorescence an erect flowering stem with sheaths, rising from corm, a loosely flowered raceme of twenty to fifty purple and green flowers; floral bract lanceolate, 20 mm. long; dorsal sepal green to purplish, oblanceolate, lateral sepals red-brown to green, oblique; petals maroon, obovate; lip hinged to base of column foot, three-lobed, green or purplish maroon, lateral lobes upcurving, median lobe downcurved with wavy margin, reddish purple with two lamellae; column green, slightly winged with compressed column foot, 14 mm. long; anther terminal; ovary slender, pedicellate, 2 cm. long.
A fairly common orchid in the southern half of Florida, growing in various wet habitats from swamps and seepage areas to roadside ditches. Flowers from July to September in central Florida.

Smooth-Lipped Eulophia *Eulophia ecristata* (Fernald) Ames
50–170 cm., terrestrial, glabrous; leaves two to four, yellowish green, pleated, linear-lanceolate; inflorescence an erect scape with enveloping sheaths, moderately dense raceme of ten to thirty yellow and dark purple flowers; floral bracts lanceolate, longer than flowers; sepals and petals pale yellow, oblong, converging over lip; lip deeply three-lobed, ovate, lateral lobes truncate, curved upward, median lobe obtuse, slightly concave at base, deep purple-brown with greenish yellow margin, smooth without lamellae; column short, green; anther terminal; ovary stout, pedicellate. Distinguished from *E. alta* by flower color, lack of lamellae on lip, and lip flat not deeply concave. A southeastern species found in North and South Carolina, Florida, and Louisiana. Grows usually in dry areas, woodlands, open rocky soils, dry fields, and edges of swamps. Flowers from July to September.

Bee Swarm Orchids *Cyrtopodium*

About twenty species of this genus are found in South America, two of which occur in Florida. Characterized by large fusiform pseudobulbs sheathed by pleated leaves; many-flowered branching stem; flower parts large and spreading; column with curved foot to which three-lobed lip is attached, lateral lobes upcurving, median lobe with verrucose margin; column with terminal anther and pair of waxy pollinia.

Bee Swarm Orchid *Cyrtopodium punctatum* (Linnaeus) Lindley
80–100 cm., epiphytic, robust; pseudobulbs from short, thick rhizome, fusiform and segmented, up to 30 cm. long; leaves up to eight or ten with sheathing bracts below; inflorescence a stout flowering stalk from base of pseudobulb, branched, with up to forty showy flowers; floral bracts oblong, undulate, yellowish with purplish brown blotching, up to 10 cm. long; sepals oblong, undulate, yellowish green with purple markings; petals broadly oblong, yellow with few brown spots; lip three-lobed with narrow base joining column foot, lateral lobes rounded, red-brown, upcurved, median lobe yellow with orange verrucose margin, small nodular callosity in center of lip; column yellow, 7 mm. long, with foot; anther terminal; ovary slender, pedicellate, 4 cm. long. Often called cowhorn orchid on account of its pseudobulbs; these and distinctive color pattern make identification easy. Now an uncommon species. Grows in inaccessible forests and swamps in southern Florida. Flowers from March to May.

(Continued on next text page)

Bee-Swarm Orchid

C. punctatum

Smooth-Lipped Eulophia

E. ecristata

Anderson's Cyrtopodium

C. andersonii

Thick-Leaved Maxillaria

M. crassifolia

Anderson's Cyrtopodium *Cyrtopodium andersonii* (Lambert ex Andrews) R. Brown in Aiton
100–160 cm., terrestrial, leafy; pseudobulbs very large, up to 1 m. long, fusiform, segmented; leaves up to twelve, from ovate bracts below to linear above; inflorescence from base of pseudobulb, stout, branching with many yellow flowers; floral bract 5 cm. long, wavy, yellowish green; sepals elliptic, spreading, yellowish green; petals obovate, yellow; lip three-lobed, sessile, from orange-yellow to orange, lateral lobes upcurved, median lobe expanded with concave base; column 6 mm.; anther terminal; ovary pedicellate, 3 cm. long.

Only recently recorded from the Everglades in southern Florida; extremely rare. Flowers during April and May in Florida.

Maxillarias *Maxillaria*

A New World group of some 250 species, some of which are epiphytic, others terrestrial, one species occurring in southern Florida. Characterized by compressed pseudobulbs partly enfolded by leaf-bearing sheaths; one or more flowering stalks, each with a single flower, borne in axils of sheaths; sepals and petals free; lip three-lobed or entire, inserted into a short column foot, center of lip with variously modified callus; anther terminal; four waxy pollinia.

Thick-Leaved Maxillaria *Maxillaria crassifolia* (Lindley) Reichenbach filius
25–40 cm., epiphytic, fan-shaped; pseudobulbs compressed, enveloped by five or six leaf sheaths, leaves two to six, linear, dark green, central leaf from apex of pseudobulb; inflorescence one to three pale yellow flowers, each borne on short stalk from leaf-sheath axil; floral bracts hidden from view, 1 cm. long; sepals oblong; petals oblanceolate; lip shallowly three-lobed, elliptic, lateral lobes mere bulges in outline, center of lip with longitudinal callus; column 1 cm. long with short column foot and terminal anther.

Distinguished by its small yellow flowers growing from axils of leaf sheaths. First discovered in southern Florida in 1934, known from interior of Fahkahatchee Swamp; very uncommon and elusive. Flowers from September to January.

Ionopsis *Ionopsis*

A group of about ten epiphytic orchids found in Central and South America, with one species occurring in southern Florida. Characterized by narrow, rigid leaves originating from small pseudobulb; many flowers in a lax panicle that grows from base of pseudobulb; dorsal sepal and petals free, lateral sepals behind large lip; lip narrow at base spreading into two large lobes, colorful and conspicuous; column short with terminal anther.

Delicate Ionopsis *Ionopsis utricularioides* (Swartz) Lindley
10–75 cm., epiphytic, leafy; pseudobulbs small, ellipsoid, concealed by leaf sheaths; leaves one to five, linear, rigid, keeled, up to 15 cm. long; inflorescence a flowering stem up to 50 cm. long, branching, with up to seventy pink flowers with marked violet veining; floral bracts small, 2 mm. long; sepals elliptic, lateral sepals united at base behind lip; petals obovate, oblique; lip spreading broadly into two lobes, pink with violet veins, joined to base of column, pair of erect lamellae toward base of lip; column short, 2 mm. long with terminal anther; ovary slender, pedicellate, 10 mm. long.

Easily recognized by its fan-shaped spreads of stiff green leaves and conspicuous pink lip. Confined to southern Florida, where it is still a common species. Grows on tree limbs in forest areas, hammocks, and swamps. Flowers from December to April.

Delicate Ionopsis

I. utricularioides

Spider Orchid

B. caudata

Spider Orchid *Brassia*

Some fifty species of this genus are found in Central and South America, with one species known from Florida. Epiphytic, having flattened pseudobulbs with one to three leathery leaves. Extremely showy flowers, with characteristic long attenuated sepals, borne on a peduncle from axil of pseudobulb; lip simple, usually a pair of lamellae toward base; column short with a terminal anther.

Spider Orchid *Brassia caudata* (Linnaeus) Lindley

30–50 cm., epiphytic; pseudobulbs ovoid, smooth, compressed, up to 12 cm. long; leaves two, oblanceolate, glossy green, spreading from apex of pseudobulb; inflorescence a flowering stalk up to 40 cm. long, rising from axil of leaf sheath at base of pseudobulb, a well-spaced raceme of up to fifteen flowers with long, slender floral parts, horizontal or pendent; floral bract lanceolate, 10 mm. long, yellowish green; sepals and petals, the former greatly lengthened, yellowish with irregular brownish markings, free and spreading; lip diamond-shaped, acuminate, pale yellow with red-brown spots, pair of lamellae with a tooth in front of each; column erect, 3.5 mm. long, yellowish green with a terminal anther; ovary slender, angled, pedicellate.

Species unmistakable with its long filiform sepals. A very uncommon species found on trunks and limbs of trees in hammocks of southern Florida, mainly in Everglades National Park. Flowers during May and June.

Oncidiums *Oncidium*

A very large genus of over five hundred species, represented in Florida by four species. Characterized by pseudobulbs ranging from large to rudimentary; leaves from thin and membranous to thick and leathery; inflorescence a simple raceme or a branched stem; flowers colorful and showing great variation; sepals and petals usually free and spreading; lip generally three-lobed, median lobe with various fleshy lamellae toward base; anther terminal.

Spread-Eagle Oncidium *Oncidium carthagenense* (Jacquin) Swartz

1–2 m., epiphytic, leafy; pseudobulbs rudimentary, concealed by sheaths; bearing a single leathery green leaf; inflorescence a flowering stem branched with up to sixty colorful flowers; floral bract lanceolate, 5 mm. long; sepals and petals from suborbicular to spatulate; lip three-lobed, lateral lobes basal, median lobe expanded, undulate, toward base verrucose, pink; column short, 3 mm. long, winged, pink, with terminal anther; ovary slender, pedicellate, 2 cm. long.

Can be recognized by single leaf and median lobe of lip less than 1.5 cm. wide. First collected in 1916 in Monroe County, Florida, and never found again. Feared to be extinct in the United States. Flowers from April to September.

Florida Oncidium *Oncidium floridanum* Ames

1–2.5 m., epiphytic or terrestrial; pseudobulb ovoid, compressed, partly concealed by two or three leaf-bearing sheaths; leaves two or three, linear, borne at summit of pseudobulb; inflorescence a much-branched flowering stem carrying up to eighty green, yellow, and brown flowers; floral bracts lanceolate, 6 mm. long; sepals and petals elliptic, undulate, yellowish green marked with brown, spreading; lip three-lobed, lateral lobes basal, median lobe yellow, expanded, about as wide as distance across lateral lobes, suborbicular with sharp point at apex, toward base a central ridge and several pairs of callosities; column 5 mm. long, narrowed in center, winged, with terminal anther; ovary slender, pedicellate, 24 mm. long.

Can be recognized by its prominent pseudobulb topped by several leaves and by its yellow lip. Species not uncommon but very local. Grows in hammocks in humus terrestrially or as an epiphytic at base of trees and on stumps; sometimes in large clumps. Known only from southern Florida. Flowers from May to August, but blooms may be found at other times.

Spread-Eagle Oncidium

O. carthagenense

Florida Oncidium

O. floridanum

Dingy Flowered Oncidium *Oncidium luridum* Lindley

1.5–2 m., epiphytic; pseudobulbs concealed by sheaths, broad but short, 1 cm. long, giving rise to single thick, leathery leaf; inflorescence a flowering stem, branched, arched, with up to fifty glossy, brown, yellow, or green flowers blotched with red-brown; floral bract lanceolate, 8 mm. long; sepals and petals broadly spatulate, undulate, spreading, yellow with red-brown spotting; lip three-lobed, lateral lobes basal, small, median lobe broadly expanded, undulate, same color as sepals and petals; column 6 mm. long, winged, with terminal anther; ovary slender, pedicellate, 24 mm. long.

Can be distinguished by its solitary leaf and width of lateral lip lobes more than 1.5 cm. An uncommon species in forests and hammocks in southern Florida, nowadays mainly in Everglades National Park. Grows on branches and tree trunks. Flowers from December to June with peak during May.

Florida Variegated Oncidium *Oncidium bahamense* Nash ex Britton & Millspaugh

50–80 cm., terrestrial or semi-epiphytic, fan-shaped; pseudobulb small, hidden by basal leaves; leaves four to eight, one leaf from apex of pseudobulb, rigid, green, with finely serrated edges; inflorescence up to three flowering stems rising erect from leaf axils, 50 cm. long with up to twenty-five white and mauve flowers that vary greatly in shape and color; floral bract lanceolate, 2 mm. long; dorsal sepal spatulate, mottled green and brown, lateral sepals lanceolate and fused, hidden behind lip; petals spatulate with pointed tips, white marked with purple or yellow-brown, tip white; lip three-lobed, lateral lobes white, median lobe expanded, white; various-colored callosities toward base; column 6 mm. long, anther terminal; ovary slender, pedicellate, 22 mm. long. Distinguished by its very small pseudobulb, fan of serrated leaves, and mainly white lip. Rare in southern Florida where it occurs in hammocks and forested areas, growing in humus or on stumps. Flowers during May and June.

Leochilus *Leochilus*

A small genus of about fifteen species found from Mexico to South America; one species found rarely in Florida. Epiphytic; slightly flattened, ovoid pseudobulbs with one or two leaves from apex; flowering stem from leaf axil at base of pseudobulb; flowers small and few in number; sepals and petals small, spreading, often with lateral sepals connate behind lip; lip entire or three-lobed, adnate to base of column; column short; anther terminal.

Large-Lipped Leochilus *Leochilus labiatus* (Swartz) Kuntze

12–20 cm., epiphytic; pseudobulb ovoid to suborbicular, compressed, with sheathing leaves; leaves two or three, one borne at apex of pseudobulb; inflorescence a slender flower stalk, about 12 cm. long, sometimes branched, with three to six fleshy yellowish or greenish flowers marked with maroon-red; floral bract ovate, 4 mm. long; dorsal sepal elliptic, lateral sepals fused along half their length, half hidden behind lip; petals elliptic; lip entire, elliptic, with two-lobed callus, base concave and pubescent, 6 mm. long; column small, 1.5 mm. long, anther terminal; ovary slender, pedicellate.

Confined to southern Florida, where it is rare and local, growing in Fahkahatchee Swamp and perhaps elsewhere, often among other epiphytic plants. Flowers during April and May.

Dingy-Flowered Oncidium

O. luridum

Large-Lipped Leochilus

L. labiatus

Florida Variegated Oncidium

O. bahamense

Macradenia *Macradenia*

A small genus of about a dozen epiphytic species of the American tropics and subtropics; one species found in Florida. Epiphytic with slender pseudobulb; leaves fleshy; inflorescence a flowering stem bearing loose raceme of small flowers; sepals and petals free; lip three-lobed, continuous with base of column; column without foot; anther erect.

Trinidad Macradenia *Macradenia lutescens* R. Brown

20–45 cm., epiphytic; pseudobulb slender, concealed by sheaths, at apex producing one leaf, oblong-lanceolate, acute; inflorescence a stem rising from base of pseudobulb, pendent with laxly flowered raceme of salmon-buff flowers with reddish markings; floral bracts lanceolate, 3–11 mm. long; dorsal sepal elliptic, concave, lateral sepals oblong-elliptic; petals similar, slightly falcate; lip three-lobed, lateral lobes incurved, embracing column, median lobe linear-lanceolate, strongly recurved and pendent, margins revolute, three ridges toward base; column 8 mm. long, toothed and lobed at apex; ovary slender, stalked.

Can be recognized by its solitary leaf and pendent, salmon-colored flowers in a raceme. An uncommon species that grows on lower branches and trunks of trees in southern peninsular Florida. Flowers during December and January.

Harris's Pygmy Orchid *Harrisella*

A tiny epiphytic orchid that belongs in the small genus *Harrisella;* three species found in the American tropics one ranging into Florida. Plant is leafless, consisting of a group of chlorophyllous roots; inflorescence a few-flowered raceme of tiny nonresupinate flowers; sepals and petals free; lip base produced into globose spur; column short; anther terminal.

Harris's Pygmy Orchid *Harrisella porrecta* (Reichenbach filius) Fawcett & Rendle

3–5 cm., epiphytic, leafless; cluster of grayish green roots; inflorescence up to six very slender racemes bearing one to six minute yellowish nonresupinate flowers; floral bract 1 mm. long; sepals and petals elliptic; lip uppermost, broadly ovate and concave, base expanded into globose spur; column winged; anther terminal; ovary stout.

Can be recognized by tiny size, greenish yellow color, and globose spur. Locally not uncommon in southern Florida, where it often grows on branches of orange trees. Flowers during August and September.

Thick-Rooted Orchid *Campylocentrum*

A group of some forty species in the American tropics, one of which occurs in Florida. Plant consists of a cluster of thick, wide chlorophyllous roots from a slender stem; flowers borne on short, distichous spikes, often pendent; floral parts free but not spreading; lip with curved spur; column short with terminal anther.

Thick-Rooted Orchid *Campylocentrum pachyrrhizum* (Reichenbach filius) Rolfe

30–50 cm., epiphytic, leafless; numerous wide, compressed grayish roots, 4–5 mm. wide; inflorescence a pendent raceme up to 3.5 cm. long with twenty to twenty-five small orange and pink flowers arranged in two ranks; floral bract cordate, 2 mm. long; sepals elliptic, yellowish brown; petals elliptic, white with pink tinge; lip whitish pink, three-lobed, lateral lobes triangular, revolute, median lobe acuminate, base dilated into curved saccate spur; column very small with terminal yellow anther and two green pollinia; ovary sessile, 1 mm. long.

Can be recognized by its lack of leaves and by its pendent flower stem. A very uncommon species recorded from the Fahkahatchee Swamp in southern Florida. Flowers during September and October.

(Continued on next text page)

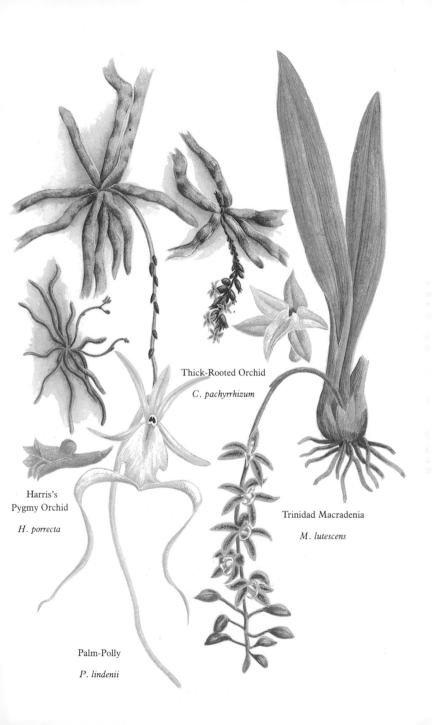

Thick-Rooted Orchid

C. pachyrrhizum

Harris's
Pygmy Orchid

H. porrecta

Trinidad Macradenia

M. lutescens

Palm-Polly

P. lindenii

Palm-Polly *Polyrrhiza*

In many ways one of the most striking of North American orchids. One of five species found in the West Indies. Leafless; thick chlorophyllous roots; large flowers with sepals and petals free and spreading; lip with long spur; column short with terminal anther. Names Ghost Orchid and Jumping Frog Orchid sometimes given to this genus.

Palm-Polly *Polyrrhiza lindenii* (Lindley) Cogniaux

10–30 cm., epiphytic, leafless; plant consists of a cluster of numerous thick greenish roots, 3–5 mm. wide, radiating from stem; inflorescence a flowering stem up to 25 cm. long with up to eight relatively large creamy white flowers with very long twisted lip lobes; sepals and petals lanceolate, whitish green, free and spreading; lip three-lobed, median lobe triangular, tapering into two elongated, twisted lobes 6.5 cm. long with a small tooth between them; base produced into long slender spur 12 cm. long; column short and thick, 2 mm. long, winged, with terminal anther; ovary slender, pedicellate, 30 mm. long.

Leafless state and flower structure render this species unmistakable. A local and uncommon plant in the hammocks and swamp forests of southern Florida; grows on branches and tree trunks. Flowers from April to August with peak in July.

GLOSSARY OF BOTANICAL TERMS

Acuminate: becoming gradually narrower toward the tip

Acute: with a tip that narrows abruptly to a sharp point

Albino: plant in which the flowers are lacking color pigments

Alternate: term applied to leaves that are attached at different levels along a stem, not opposite one another

Anther: that part of the stamen containing the pollen; usually divided longitudinally into two parts

Anthesis: time during which a flower is in bloom

Apex, apical: the tip or topmost point of a structure

Appendage: part attached to another larger structure

Articulate: joint; jointed

Attenuate: tapering gradually

Auricle: projecting lobe at the base of leaf, petal, or lip

Axil: upper angle where a leaf joins the stem

Bi-: prefix meaning two or twice

Bifid, bilobed: cleft in two no farther than to the middle

Bifurcate: forked, with two equal branches

Bog: swampy habitat on wet acid, peaty soil

Bract: small leaflike or scalelike structure from axil of which a flower stalk often arises

Bracteole: small bract arising close under flower or on its pedicel

Bulbil: tiny bulblike organ, growing at tip of leaf, which breaks off to form new plant

Bursicle: pouchlike flap covering the sticky disc (viscidium) and preventing it from drying; pushed back by an insect visiting the flower

Campanulate: bell-shaped

Capsule: dry fruit formed from two or more fused carpels; splits open when ripe to release seeds

Carpel: one of the sections of the female part of the flower, in orchids fused together into the fruit.

Caudicle: the lower stalklike part of the pollinium, connecting the pollen masses to the viscidium

Cauline: leaf borne along the stem

Chlorophyll: green coloring matter in plants

Ciliate: fringed with hair along the margin

Claw: stalklike basal part of the lip; not present in many orchids

Cleistogamous: self-fertilized in the unopened flower.

Column: the structure in the center of an orchid flower formed by the fusion of stigma and stamens; shape varies in different orchids

Column foot: basal extension of the column

Connate: united

Connivent: converging

Cordate: heart-shaped

Coriaceous: leathery in texture

Corm: enlarged fleshy base of a stem, bulblike but solid and different in structure

Corymb: flowers clustered on the same level

Deciduous: not bearing green leaves throughout the year

Deflexed: bent downward

Dehiscent: splitting open, as in dry orchid capsules, to allow the seeds to escape

Dentate: toothed

Downy: with a covering of soft hairs

Dune: habitat of wind-blown sand, usually rich in lime, with damp hollows called slacks that support vegetation

Ecology: the study of plants and animals in relation to their environment

Elliptic: oval, narrowing to a rounded end

Endemic: native of and confined to a given area or region

Entire: whole, without teeth, lobes, or indentations

Epichile: outer section of the lip in those species in which lip is divided into two distinct parts by constriction of the middle, as in the genera *Epipactis* and *Cephalanthera*

Epiphytic: growing on another plant but not parasitic

Falcate: sickle-shaped

Fen: wet habitat on calcareous soils, not acid as is a bog

Fertile: capable of bearing viable fruit

Filament: threadlike stalk of the stamen bearing the anthers

Filiform: threadlike or very slender

Foliaceous: resembling a leaf in texture and appearance

Form: slight variant of a species, usually occurring sporadically

Free: not joined together

Fugacious: withering or falling before flowers open

Fusiform: shaped like a spindle

Galea: a helmet or hood-shaped formation

Genus (plural **genera**: term used in classification for a group of closely related species; A number of genera form a family; generic name is first part of a plant's scientific name, e.g., *Cypripedium* (genus) *acaule* (species)

Glabrous: smooth, without hairs

Globose: globular, globe-shaped, spherical

Habit: general appearance of a plant

Habitat: conditions of environment in which a plant grows; factors involved include climate, soil, supply of water, altitude, associated plants, etc.

Heath: habitat of acid soils with characteristic plants such as heaths and heathers

Herbs: fleshy, nonwoody plants

Hispid: having coarse, stiff hairs

Humus: decomposing organic matter in the soil

Hyaline: thin and translucent

Hybrid: offspring resulting from the cross-breeding of a species or hybrid with another species or hybrid and showing some characteristics of each parent

Hybrid swarm: large numbers of hybrid plants growing together, showing varying characteristics of the two parents

Hymenoptera: insects belonging to the family Hymenoptera, including wasps, bees, ants, sawflies, and ichneumons, some of which are involved in the fertilization of certain orchids

Hypochile: the basal section of the lip where the lip is divided into two distinct parts, as in the genera *Epipactis* and *Cephalanthera*

Inferior: below; orchids have an inferior ovary, i.e., one situated below the flower

Inflated: blown-up, bladderlike

Inflorescence: the flowering section of a plant

Internode: that part of the stem between two nodes; the section of stem between leaves

Involute: rolled inward

Irregular flower: not symmetrical; all orchids are irregular flowers

Keeled: with a raised ridge

Labellum: another name for the lip; the lower inner perianth segment, usually projecting downward; may be entire, two-, three-, or four-lobed

Lamella: laterally flattened ridge

Lanceolate: Spear- or lance-shaped, tapering toward apex, several times longer than wide

Lateral: borne on each side

Lax: loose and spreading as opposed to densely packed or dense

Linear: nearly parallel-sided; long and narrow

Lingulate: tongue-shaped

Lip: modified median petal in an orchid flower, usually differing markedly in size, color, and form from the other two petals; the labellum

Littoral: on seashore or near the sea

Lobe: any segment or division of an organ; e.g., a three-lobed lip is divided into three segments

Maculate: spotted

Marsh: water-logged ground but not on peat

Membranous: thin, dry, like parchment or paper

Mentum: rounded or curved projection formed by lower section of lip and adjacent floral segments

Midrib: central vein of leaf, often raised

Moniliform: resembling a string of beads

Monocarpic: flowering once and then dying

Monotypic: having only one exponent; e.g., a genus with but one species

Montane: pertaining to mountains

Morphology: the study of the structure, form, and appearance of plants

Mycorrhiza: the association of a fungus with the roots or other parts of a plant

Mycorrhizome: the initial plant body produced following germination of an orchid seed; always infected with an appropriate fungus

Nectar: sweet substance produced by many plants and attractive to insects

Nectary: secreting nectar, in orchids often part of the lip, e.g., the spur

Net-veined: a leaf in which veins are not all parallel

Node: point of origin of leaves on a stem ·

Nonresupinate: orchids in which the lip is directed upward

Oblong: elongated but relatively wide, e.g., a leaf with nearly parallel sides

Obovate: as **Ovate** but with the broadest part toward the apex

Obtuse: blunt or rounded at end

Opposite: leaves growing in pairs opposite one another along a stem

Oval: broadly elliptic

Ovary: the base of the reproductive organ (pistil) containing the embryonic seeds; ovary always situated below rest of flower in orchids

Ovate: shaped like the outline of an egg

Palmate: divided with fingerlike lobes; e.g., some orchid tubers

Panicle: a branching inflorescence

Papillose: having many small projections

Pedicel: the stalk of a single flower

Peduncle: the common stalk of a cluster of flowers

Pellucid: clear, almost transparent

Pendulous: drooping or hanging

Perennial: a plant that survives for more than two years, usually flowering each year

Perianth: the outer, nonreproductive parts of an orchid flower, comprising three outer segments called sepals, and three inner segments, the petals

Petaloid: petal-like

Petals: the three inner parts of the perianth in an orchid flower; the two simple petals on each side and the median petal usually modified and termed the lip or labellum

Pistil: the female reproductive organ, comprising style, stigma, and ovary

Plicate: folded lengthwise into pleats

Pollen: small grains that contain the male reproductive cells

Pollinium (plural **pollinia**): a mass of pollen grains held together by threads or adhesives

Polymorphic: variable, having more than one form

Pseudobulb: swelling at base of stem resembling a bulb; usually serves as a water storage organ

Pubescent: with soft downy hairs

Pyramidal: pyramid-shaped

Pyriform: pear-shaped

Raceme: an elongated inflorescence arranged singly along a stem, each flower on its own stalk; youngest flowers at the apex

Racemose: having flowers in a raceme-type inflorescence

Recurved: bent backward or downward in a curve

Reflexed: bent abruptly backward or downward

Resupinate: those orchids in which the lip is directed downward

Reticulated: net-veined, with the lateral veins connected by small veins like the meshes of a net

Revolute: margins of structure (leaf, sepals, or petals) rolled backward toward center

Rhizome: a rootlike stem growing on or below the ground with roots growing downward and leaves and shoots upward

Ribbed: with the leaf veins prominent

Rosette: leaf arrangement at ground level radiating from base of stem

Rostellum: a small beak; the slender extension from the upper edge of the stigma; the sterile third stigma of an orchid flower

Saccate: pouch-shaped

Saprophyte; saprophytic: a plant that derives its nourishment from dead organic matter; without green leaves

Scale: a thin, dry flap of tissue, usually a modified leaf

Scapose: leafless stalk

Secund: flowers in a row along one side of stem

Sepals: the three outer sections of the orchid flower, the upper or dorsal sepal and one on each side, the lateral sepals

Sessile: without a stalk

Sheath: the base of a leaf, which envelops the stem; lower leaves usually consist entirely of sheath, the leaf blade not being developed

Sinuate: with outline of margin strongly wavy

Spatulate: spoon-shaped

Species: a unit of classification indicating populations of similar plants that interbreed and produce fertile progeny; related species are grouped under the heading of genus

Spike: elongated flower cluster; flowers stalkless or nearly so

Spur: a hollow tubular extension of the orchid lip; often containing nectar

Stamen: one of the pollen-bearing male reproductive organs of a flower

Staminode: an infertile or rudimentary stamen without pollen

Stigma: the part of the female organ that receives the male pollen

Stolon: horizontal stem spreading below ground, which roots at the tip to give rise to a new plant

Subspecies: the unit of classification below species; often used to denote morphologically distinct geographical populations that are capable of interbreeding freely if brought together and are therefore included in the same species

Succulent: fleshy, juicy, and usually thickened

Symbiosis: the living together of dissimilar organisms with benefit to both

Taxonomy: the classification of plants and animals in systematic order

Terrestrial: growing in the ground and supported by soil

Toothed: with small triangular or rounded projections along margin of lip

Truncate: having the end shaped as if cut off

Tuber: a fleshy swollen underground stem or root formed annually; a food storage organ capable of producing new growtn

Tuberculate: covered with knobby projections

Undulate: wavy

Unifoliate: one-leaved

Variety: a subdivision of a species differing from typical plants in a few unimportant characteristics; usually without special geographical distribution

Vein: a thread of fibrovascular tissue in a leaf or other organ

Verrucose: covered with tubercles

Viscidium: a sticky disc connected to the pollinium, enabling it to stick to an insect's body and be carried away to another flower

CHECKLIST OF THE ORCHIDS
OF NORTH AMERICA

For those who may wish to keep a life list of the Orchids they discover.

SELECTED BIBLIOGRAPHY

Ames, O. *An Enumeration of the Orchids of the United States and Canada*. Boston: American Orchid Society, 1924.

Alexander, T. R., R. W. Burnett, and H. S. Zim. *Botany*. A Golden Nature Guide. New York: Golden Press, 1970.

Britton, N. L. and A. Brown. *An Illustrated Flora of the Northern States and Canada*. 3 vols. New York: Scribner, 1896–98.

Britton, N. L. *Flora of Bermuda*. New York: Hafner, 1918.

Case, F. W. *Orchids of the Western Great Lakes Region*. Bloomfield Hills, Mich.: Cranbrook Institute of Science, 1964.

Clark, L. J. *Wild Flowers of British Columbia*. Sidney, B.C.: Grays Publishing, 1973.

Correll, D. S. *Native Orchids of North America*. Waltham, Mass.: Chronica Botanica, 1950.

Curtis, J. T. "Some Native Orchids of the Lake Superior Region." *American Orchid Society Bulletin* (1941).

Duperrex, A. *Orchids of Europe*. London: Blandford Press, 1961.

Ettlinger, D. M. T. *British and Irish Orchids: A Field Guide*. London: Macmillan, 1976.

Godfery, M. J. and H. M. Godfery. *Monograph and Iconograph of Native British Orchidaceae*. Cambridge: Cambridge University Press, 1933.

Green, E. I. "Wild Orchids of the Northeastern States." *American Orchid Society Bulletin* 37 (1968).

Hulten, E. *Flora of Alaska and Neighboring Territories*. Stanford, Calif.: Stanford University Press, 1968.

————. "Flora of Alaska and Yukon." Lund: Lund University, 1943, Arsski II. Sec. 2.

Luer, C. A. *The Native Orchids of Florida*. New York: New York Botanical Garden, 1972.

————. *The Native Orchids of the United States and Canada excluding Florida*. New York: New York Botanical Garden, 1975.

Morris, F. and E. A. Eames. *Our Wild Orchids*. New York: Scribner, 1929.

Niehaus, T. F. and C. L. Ripper. *Field Guide to Pacific States Wildflowers*. Boston: Houghton Mifflin, 1976.

Peterson, R. T. and M. McKenny. *Field Guide to the Flowers of Northeastern and North-central North America*. Boston: Houghton Mifflin, 1968.

Petrie, W. *Guide to Orchids of North America*, Vancouver, B.C.: Hancock House, 1981.

Rickett, H. W. *The New Field Book of American Wild Flowers*. New York: Putnam, 1963.

Rickett, H. W. *The Wild Flowers of the United States*. 6 vols. New York: McGraw-Hill, 1966–73.

Shuttleworth, Floyd S., H. S. Zim, and Gordon W. Dillon. *Orchids*. A Golden Nature Guide. New York: Golden Press, 1970.

Summerhayes, V. S. *Wild Orchids of Britain*. London: Collins, 1951.

Sundermann, H. *Europaeische und mediterrane Orchideen*. Hildesheim: Brücke-Verlag Kurt Schmersow, 1975.

Szczawinski, A. F. *The Orchids of British Columbia*. Victoria, B.C.: British Columbia Provincial Museum, 1959.

Van der Pijl, L. and C. H. Dodson. *Orchid Flowers: Their Pollination and Evolution*. Miami: University of Miami Press, 1966.

Wallace, J. E. "The Orchids of Maine." *University of Maine Bulletin* 53 (1951).

Williams, J. G., A. E. Williams, and N. Arlott. *A Field Guide to the Orchids of Britain and Europe*. London: Collins, 1978.

INDEX

Page references for illustrations are in italics.